PRAISE FOR *CALM INSPIRATION*

Calm Inspiration, with its insights and lessons, has something to offer each of us as we pursue our personal odyssey of social-emotional growth and discovery. Through this heartfelt collection of entries, Jenny reveals her own journey of self-discovery and human connection. As I read, I was repeatedly inspired by Jenny's honesty, frailty, optimism, and personal growth. Her prose provoked, in me, a spectrum of emotions and connections and some ah-ha moments, and most importantly, reminded me of many of my own life lessons that I hold dear.   *Karen DeSpirito, Ph.D., School Psychologist*

Jenny has truly changed our family for the better. She's incredibly relatable and has a way of helping us see that we're not alone in dealing with big emotions. I've learned so much from her, and so have my two children. Now we are all much calmer and more equipped to handle the everyday stresses that come our way.
  Sara Horvet, Parent

Gathering from a well of lived experience, professional expertise, and humility, Jenny has the ability to not only share her stories but also to illuminate the path toward emotional resilience and self-awareness. This book is more than a personal narrative; it is a heartfelt exploration of the challenges we all face and the powerful lessons learned along the way.   *Becky Midler, MA, LMHC*

calm inspiration

real life lessons of
social emotional learning
for educators, parents,
and caregivers

jenny gaynor

Calm Inspiration: Real Life Lessons of Social Emotional
Learning for Educators, Parents, and Caregivers
Copyright © 2025 Jenny Gaynor

Produced and printed by Stillwater River Publications.
All rights reserved. Written and produced in the United
States of America. This book may not be reproduced
or sold in any form without the expressed, written
permission of the author and publisher.

Visit our website at
www.StillwaterPress.com
for more information.

First Stillwater River Publications Edition.

ISBN: 978-1-965733-15-8

1 2 3 4 5 6 7 8 9 10
Written by Jenny Gaynor.
Cover & interior book design by Matthew St. Jean.
Published by Stillwater River Publications,
West Warwick, RI, USA.

Publisher's Cataloging-in-Publication
(Provided by Cassidy Cataloguing Services, Inc.)
Names: Gaynor, Jenny, author.
Title: Calm inspiration : real life lessons of social emotional learning
for educators, parents, and caregivers / Jenny Gaynor.
Description: First Stillwater River Publications edition. |
West Warwick, RI, USA : Stillwater River Publications, [2025]
Identifiers: ISBN: 978-1-965733-15-8
Subjects: LCSH: Social learning—Anecdotes. | Affective education—
Anecdotes. | Self-consciousness (Awareness) | Inspiration. |
Educators—Psychology. | Parents—Psychology. | Caregivers—
Psychology. | LCGFT: Self-help publications.
Classification: LCC: HQ783 .G39 2025 |
DDC: 303.32—dc23

*The views and opinions expressed in this book are
solely those of the author and do not necessarily reflect
the views and opinions of the publisher.*

*To JAG, JCG, and EKG for all you offer me every day!
You give me so much to be grateful for, and I love you
more than you know!*

contents

Foreword..*xiii*

Part 1: Introducing Calm...Inspiration!
1. It's Time to Share My Story................................... 1
2. A Tricky Riddle? Or Simply Fate? 7
3. I'm All In 13

Part 2: Lessons in Habits, Life Changes, and Goals
4. A Beginner's Mind..21
5. This is Me..25
6. Crafting Your Order..31
7. The Problem with My Habits 36
8. Not Everything You Love is Good for You 40
9. There's a Gift in Gray Chin Hairs..........................45

Part 3: Lessons in Relationships
10. What Do You Know...53
11. We Are All Connected 57
12. Friends Are Nature's Way of Taking Care of Us 61
13. Far (But Not So Distant) Friends 67
14. Dirty Chocolate..71
15. You Couldn't Pay Me 75

Part 4: Lessons in Family

16. In the Spirit of Thanksgiving... 81
17. The Universe and the Message She Sends 85
18. Gotta Love Teen Spirit 90
19. Take Credit for the Good Things, Too! 93
20. Better to Have Loved and Lost... 96

Part 5: Lessons in Roadblocks

21. The Balance 103
22. It Doesn't Have to Be this way.. 106
23. A Follow up...with Gratitude 114
24. The Worst!..117
25. Where Crisis Can Lead Us... 125
26. Overthinkers Anonymous 129
27. Perfectly Imperfect 135
28. You're a Mean One, Mr. Grinch 142
29. Looking for Glimmers 146
30. Emotions Are My Jam... 151
31. Reading My Labels 159

Part 6: Lessons in Indulgences

32. My Cat is a Life Coach 167
33. Little Rainbows Everywhere 171
34. Buy the Latte 175
35. My Cheesy TV Obsession 178
36. Things We Can Learn From My Favorite
    Reality TV Show... 181

Part 7: Lessons in Holidays and Seasons

37. Putting Up with Winter 189
38. Resolutions Are a Thing of the Past 192
39. A Gift from the Heart 196
40. Emerging from My Hibernation.................................... 201

41. Slowing Down, Not Speeding Up 206
42. Perpetual Sundays 210
43. Summer's Funeral 215

Part 8: Lessons in Managing Life's Emotions
44. The Hard Emotions 221
45. Nature Can Nurture 226
46. White Picket Fences Around Me 231
47. Kickboxing is My Anger Management 237
48. Name it To Tame It 241
49. Practice Makes Progress 246
50. Just Lose That Narrative 251
51. Practicing Positivity 255
52. To-Do, To-Don't, Or To-Be, That is the Question 262
53. The Rollercoaster is Real! 266
54. Mental Health Days 272

Postscript 275
Acknowledgments 278
About the Author 281

calm inspiration

foreword

MY NAME IS JENNY, AND I AM A FORMER PUBLIC school teacher turned SEL coach who is devoted to inspiring children and caregivers through the power of Social-Emotional Learning.

Many of us are unclear about the exact meaning of social-emotional learning, and there seems to be a lot of debate about it. The Collaborative for Academic, Social, and Emotional Learning (CASEL) defines SEL as *"the process through which all young people and adults acquire and apply the knowledge, skills, and attitudes to develop healthy identities, manage emotions and achieve personal and collective goals, feel and show empathy for others, establish and maintain supportive relationships, and make responsible and caring decisions."* CASEL has established five core competencies of SEL, which include self-management, self-awareness, social awareness, responsible decision-making, and relationship skills.

The Committee for Children says SEL is *"the process of developing the self-awareness, self-control, and interpersonal skills that are vital for school, work, and life success."* They claim that learning SEL skills helps kids, adults, and communities create a foundation for positive, long-term effects. Their research states that "there is a strong correlation between the skills taught in SEL programs and academic achievement, positive behavior, and healthier life choices."

Me? I describe SEL as *a series of life skills that we all need in order to be unequivocally human!* For a few of us, some Social-Emotional skills come naturally. But for most of us, we need to learn them through experiencing, reading, role-playing, mistake-making, discussing, creating, and more!

Through my over twenty years in public education, I taught SEL before it even had a label. As part of my routines and procedures in my classroom, I helped my students foster relationships, work collaboratively, become curious, have an open mind, express gratitude, demonstrate empathy, identify emotions, set goals, and more! And I wasn't alone in this mission. I worked with countless amazing colleagues who wanted to foster the same skills in their students, too!

As a parent of two children, I do my best to help foster SEL within my family. I help to teach my kids how to communicate effectively, resist negative social pressure, identify solutions for personal and social problems, understand other perspectives, manage emotions, take initiative, and so much more! Am I perfect at it? Nope…but like all human parents, I try. I know I'm not alone on this mission either. I live in a community full of beautiful families who want the same for their children as I want for my own!

Teaching these skills takes time, balance, and patience! And it takes a village of parents, families, neighbors, friends, schools, churches, wellness centers, doctors…get the idea? This is why I started my business, Calm Education, and decided to write this book for educators, parents, and caregivers. Even before COVID hit and shut the world down, I saw a need for us to slow down. The world can move at such a fast pace, which in turn leads us to forget how to lead with love, patience, curiosity, and without judgment. Schools are driven heavily by test scores and student academic data. Families are driven by daily agendas and hectic schedules. I have found that my purpose in this role is to help children, teachers, and families slow down and focus on what is truly important in their lives.

As a way to find stillness and time for reflection for myself, I recently re-discovered my love for writing. As a kid, I often had a pen in my hand. I invented stories, wrote poems, and chronicled my life in journals. Over time, life got in the way, and I somehow let go of all that writing. It wasn't until I decided to start the "Calm Blog" as part of my business that I remembered how much I loved it. Almost a year ago, I began writing about things happening in my life and used this writing as a tool to help me process my emotions. With the Calm Blog, I created an audience that I hoped would find value in some of my life experiences.

If you are a parent, teacher, caregiver, or human in the business of children, you are my audience. Through this book, I invite you to become curious about how you can foster SEL in your lives. I am, by no means, a perfect model for Social-Emotional Wellbeing. We are ALL human, and just like you, I have my moments. But my stories are exactly that...human and real! You don't need to read this book cover-to-cover. Simply pick it up and read the stories in any order you would like. And continue to read them again as much as you need for inspiration.

Through my anecdotes, I hope you see that there can be a lesson in everything life offers, and I hope you can use this book to inspire you to find ways to take care of yourself so you can better take care of those around you.

Enjoy and be well, my friends!

PART 1

introducing calm...
inspiration!

CHAPTER 1

it's time to share my story

AT THE END OF THE 2021-22 SCHOOL YEAR, I LEFT MY job as a public school teacher. I'm finally ready to share my story about why I made this choice.

If you didn't already know this about me, I am a former elementary educator. I taught in both public and charter schools for over twenty years in California, Massachusetts, and Rhode Island.

I enjoyed my job.

I loved my colleagues.

I adored my students.

A few years before COVID-19 hit our world, I had a little buzz in my brain telling me that it was time for me to make a shift in my world of teaching. But I was scared. Teaching in a classroom was all I knew and the only career path I'd have in my lifetime. I felt it was my calling, and I still think it was...for the time that I held that position, anyway.

In August 2020, right in the heart of the COVID pandemic, my family moved to New Zealand for my husband's job. I was fresh off teaching my students virtually, never really seeing them in person to say goodbye, and I was exhausted. Like most educators, and people for that matter, I didn't know what hit me.

My family knew four years prior that we would be moving to New Zealand, and despite what was happening in the rest of the world, I took a year's leave of absence from the classroom, packed up my family, and left! We spent nine glorious months in Aotearoa, essentially living in freedom, while the rest of my friends and family worked, taught, and lived behind masks and plexiglass shields.

We were lucky.

But I was lucky in more ways than just dodging a pandemic bullet. The year away from my classroom gave me clarity on exactly what I wanted to accomplish as an educator.

When we came home from the other side of the world, I decided to return to the classroom for the 2021-2022 school year. It didn't take me long. By October, my husband found me one day with tears streaming down my face as I formed a ball on our bed. He asked what was wrong, and I told him that life was too short for this. I didn't belong in a classroom anymore...that I still loved kids, which was why I was still doing this job. But I wanted to teach kids in a different way. I had different ideas. It was my husband who first encouraged me to make a change that would be better for me, for the children I worked with, and maybe even our community. He inspired me to see that this change could work!

Throughout that school year, I worked behind the scenes on my newly forming vision of my career. After school hours, I updated my resume, which I hadn't done in over a decade. I joined LinkedIn, which felt very foreign to me. And I started to research and apply for jobs related to education and SEL.

When that school year ended, some say I retired, but I didn't file any formal paperwork for that, and I think I'm too young to use that word.

Sometimes, I get asked if I resigned, but to me, that implies that I quit teaching, which isn't true.

I don't think I resigned, quit, or retired. I think I made a shift to a different kind of education for kids called Social Emotional Learning, or as they say in the business, "SEL."

SEL isn't new. It is something I think I have been doing with my students every day in the classroom for years. SEL is teaching kids how to be part of a community, interact with others, love themselves, show compassion for others, value their learning, and thrive.

Especially after the COVID-19 pandemic and with the increase in pressure for teachers to close gaps and increase test scores, it didn't take me long after leaving the classroom to set up Calm Education, LLC. My business is designed to help children, their families, and their teachers with social-emotional learning. I love the change of pace, making my own schedule, designing my own lessons, working with students and educators in a smaller environment, and directly seeing the fruits of my labor.

I am often asked if I miss working as a classroom teacher. I think that is like asking me if I miss being in college. Of course, I miss so many things about it…the social interactions, the fun, the rewards, the learning! But it is a thing of the past for me. I was ready to move on. I hit a point in my career when I knew that a public school classroom wasn't the place for me anymore. I knew that my talents were ready to be presented in a new way. Nature was telling me that it was time, and I listened.

I am so privileged that I was able to make this shift in my career. My husband's job funded our family enough that we could take the pay cut while I worked toward setting up this new business…for a little while, anyway. There are many times when I continue to question how I am going to make ends meet!

Many of my former colleagues tell me that they would like to do something similar but don't have the means to take the leap. They often use the phrase, "I feel stuck." Does this resonate with some of my educator friends out there? Are you feeling what some call "burnout" from education?

I am going to urge you to rephrase that thinking. Instead of saying you feel "stuck" or "burnt out," perhaps you can say...this is where you are meant to be. The universe, nature, or whatever higher power you believe in, is telling you that teaching children in a school, in a classroom, is where you belong. I know I sound cliche here, but perhaps you are a "chosen one." You are a strong educator. If we didn't have you, who else would do it?

I think I speak for many parents when I say that I am grateful there are teachers still in the classroom, teaching our children. Our children rely on people like these educators. Our children will always need someone like classroom teachers to guide them, make an impression on them, and inspire them.

I wish that I had someone who gave me better guidance when I started teaching. I had no idea of the pressures I would feel, the worries I would hold, and the stress I would be under. There were many times that I had difficulty dealing with all the emotions that teachers in a classroom feel every day. As a result, I didn't always take the best care of myself. Sometimes, I look back at my first few years of teaching and wonder how I was able to stay with it. This is **why** I host Calm Education wellness workshops for educators and staff... to help them manage their emotions in such a demanding career.

Feel free to trash or treasure this unsolicited advice I have for all of you out there working in the world of education....

If you are wondering how you are going to stick with being a teacher, molding impressionable young minds. Think back to your WHY. Why did you become a teacher in the first place? Really think about that for a little while. Sleep on it. Meditate on it. Walk with this question. Once you know the answer to this, you will know how you will stay in the classroom or shift your way of being an educator.

When thinking about shifting my career, I reflected and meditated on this question quite often. Why did I go into teaching in the first place?

It is because I love kids.

I loved being a kid.

I love hanging out with kids.

When I was younger, my summer jobs consisted of teaching kids how to swim and how to sail. It wasn't until I taught a little boy with Autism how to swim that I knew I wanted to teach kids for my life. Honestly? I wanted to save the world!

Looking back on it, I realize now that saving the world was a bit of a lofty goal. I could only take one school year, one classroom, and one student at a time to see what I could do to inspire them. Throughout my years, I felt joy when I stood in front of the classroom. I loved staying up late, putting together craft supplies for a project. I enjoyed turning my classroom into a pseudo-beach in the warmer months when I taught summer school. I couldn't wait to begin a new unit and try out new ideas and lessons. It lit me up to see students admire their own growth. There was no other career that could do that for me.

Throughout the second half of my career, I started to see a change in schools and the way I was teaching. I began to resent the weekends and late nights that I had to spend correcting. I didn't have time to put together fun craft supplies for my students. With health mandates, fear of intruders, and fire codes, I wasn't always able to turn my classroom into a fun place to learn. New units usually meant new curriculum materials, and they began to fly at me at an overwhelming rate. I wasn't able to be creative and write my own lessons because with new curriculum materials came robotic teacher scripts that I had to figure out how to make my own. When I looked at my students in my last few years of teaching, especially across a computer screen through the pandemic, I didn't see the spark that I used to be able to ignite in my students. And I realized that was because my own spark was starting to dim.

Finally, leaving my job as a public school classroom teacher for over twenty years was really hard to do. I had to go back to my WHY so many times.

Why do I want to be a teacher?
Because I love kids.
I love helping kids.
I love being around kids.

I wanted to continue to love teaching, nurturing, and being around kids. The classroom was suffocating me, making it really challenging to give children the love they deserved from their classroom teacher. This is why I decided to make the shift.

I am forever grateful that I can continue to help children and their families. I'm using what I know about learning, development, and teaching to continue to mold, inspire, and help kids see their potential! I am often asked, "How are things now that you're not teaching?" And I am quick to respond, "I still teach, just in a different way." I still identify as an educator. That is one thing about me that I know will never change....

CHAPTER 2

a tricky riddle? or simply fate?

WHAT DO TAYLOR SWIFT, GRACE LIN, SHELDON COOper, and Calm Education all have in common? No...this isn't some sort of tricky riddle! They all have to do with a crazy rabbit hole I found myself digging into the other day after a car ride with my daughter.

Let me explain....

If I am going to listen to Taylor Swift, it is usually with my daughter on our way to one of her many activities throughout the week. We listen to Taylor in the car, almost always singing along. Taylor's songs are easy to pick up on, and her words seem to appeal to everyone at every stage of life. While the tunes are catchy and fun, I particularly enjoy the poetry behind the lyrics.

The other day, we were listening to a song called "Invisible String," released on Taylor's Folklore album in 2020. There's a story in this song about someone that she fell in love with, someone she may have known previously but didn't realize the feelings for a while. She talks about the metaphorical connection she had to this person all along....through the ups and downs of other relationships. And she mentions that there may have been an "invisible string" tying the two of them together.

This made me think about one of my favorite children's authors, Grace Lin. My hands-down, all-time favorite book of hers to read aloud in my classroom was *Where the Mountain Meets the Moon*. It is possibly one of my favorite books I have ever read, let alone aloud to children.

Minli is the main character, who runs away from home to find good fortune for her poor family and village. Along the way, she meets many different characters who help her find "The Old Man of the Moon" so she can convince him to "change her destiny."

I love how Grace Lin uses different Chinese Legends to tell the story of Minli's adventures and explain the theme of connections that are "woven" throughout her experiences. In fact, based on a little bit of my research, it seems that the character of The Old Man of the Moon is inspired by the Chinese legend of Yue Lao, the God of Marriage and Love, who unites predestined couples with a silk cord.

In *Where the Mountain Meets the Moon*, Minli learns that a character in the book, The Old Man of the Moon, is in charge of tying "Red Strings of Destiny" to small clay figures. These figures represent many of the characters in the book and connect everyone together. The red strings don't necessarily represent the romantic connections that Yue Lao makes and that the original legend tells. But the idea that we are all connected by an invisible red thread to all those people we are destined to touch in some way is such a lovely idea to me, which is why I enjoy this story so much!

In fact, one year, shortly after I read this story aloud to my students, we discovered that a classmate was leaving the school year early to go visit family for an extended stay out of the country. She wasn't going to finish the school year with us or be around for the summer with her friends. She was excited about this opportunity but nervous at the same time.

As part of her going away gift, the entire class sat in a circle and tossed a red ball of yarn around. As they tossed it back and forth to their classmate, they held onto the string and shared something that they admired about their friendship. This activity was supposed to show that while we were going to miss her, our connection was always going to be there. In the end, we all looked like little clay figures holding onto The Old Man of the Moon's Red Strings of Destiny. Grace Lin's writing connected us all together in such a special way, just like the characters of her book!

So anyway...as I drove with my daughter that afternoon, Taylor Swift's poetry reminded me of this really special memory in my classroom, and I instantly fell in love with the song!

I taught and connected with students and their families for over twenty years in a public school classroom within three states and four schools. And now, I continue to make connections with students, families, and other educators in my new position as a Social Emotional Learning coach. My family jokes with me that I am like the mayor when I go out to dinner or to the grocery store. So many people say hello to me, and I often bump into students or families that I haven't seen since they left my classroom years ago. Listening to Taylor's songs made me wonder what my little clay figure would look like among the Old Man of the Moon's display! I bet it would be pretty tangled and twisted!

But that's the beauty of this story and legend! Grace Lin uses the symbolism of the Red String of Destiny in a few of her books. In each version of her red string stories, she demonstrates that the thread may stretch or tangle but may never break. Our connections to people come and go, but the impact we make on them stays. The things that we say and the things that we do for others, no matter how big or small, make a difference and an impact on the people and the world around us...on the universe!

This is a big reason why I chose the mandala as my logo for Calm Education. I want my business to help bring people together, make meaningful connections, and work toward creating a more peaceful world.

Mandala can be translated in Sanskrit to "circle" or "sacred center." The circular geometric design is used in ceremonies and meditation practices and can be found in many different cultures, such as Hindu, Buddhist, Christian, and Native American practices, just to name a few. The Mandala is believed to have originated from Buddhist monks who create elaborate mandalas made of colored sand during their ceremonial meditations. For Buddhists, mandalas represent the universe, transforming suffering into joy. And since these Buddhist monks believe that nothing in the universe is permanent, they often destroy their mandalas. Shortly after creation, the beautiful and intricate mandalas are ceremoniously placed in a river or stream. Or the grains of sand are swirled together into an unrecognizable rainbow of color.

Mandalas are meant to symbolize unity, harmony, and the interconnectedness of life, with everything in the design being connected in the center. No matter whether we are talking about mandalas, red strings of destiny, or Taylor Swift's invisible strings, the idea of everyone being connected in some way is really appealing to me! Despite our skin color, our choice of mate, our culture, our heritage, or gender...no matter what and whether we like it or not, we are connected to each other, and we are connected to nature.

I'm not the first one to be inspired by Taylor Swift's song, Invisible String. I will admit that I went down an internet rabbit hole the other day when I really started thinking about this song. In my research, I learned that TikTok has generated millions of views about the "Invisible String Theory," influenced by the queen of No. 1 hits herself! This TikTok trend tells many stories of people crossing paths millions of times before eventually coming together when the universe decides it is time.

The legends of The Old Man of the Moon and The Invisible

String Theory are fun to think about, but they are metaphorical concepts. It got me thinking about what science had to say about all of this! Where's the proof, right? If you enjoy watching *The Big Bang Theory*, you may know about the character and physicist Sheldon Cooper and his lifelong work to prove the "String Theory."

With this idea in my head, I went further down the rabbit hole of my research. I learned that "The String Theory" says reality is made up of vibrating strings, smaller than atoms and electrons. These strings vibrate, twist, and fold, producing many effects in life, including gravity. It is sometimes called "The Theory of Everything" and is meant to describe all forces and matter.

Without a true physicist's mind, I am simplifying the meaning of this theory, and my scientist friends out there reading this are probably cringing. But I do know that while it doesn't quite describe how everything is connected, The String Theory does attempt to explain why things happen the way they do.

However, I also learned that this theory is highly criticized in the math and science world. I think, eventually, even the fictional Sheldon Cooper gave up on trying to prove it. The existence of invisible strings to explain why things happen in the world is a tough one, so I'm not surprised!

All of these legends, stories, pieces of art, songs, and scientific research still leave me wondering…is everyone I've ever met or ever spent time with connected to me for a reason? Is it strings that bind us together? Or do we just call it fate, kismet, and coincidence?

Even the phrase "human nature" says it all! We are humans! We are part of nature! We are all connected to the universe in some way. And whether or not we act accordingly, what we do and what we say can make a positive difference for others. Educators, parents… and anyone working in the field with humans live and breathe this reality every day!

You might know me well. Or you might not know me at all. But the fact that you decided to spend time reading this story about my dive down rabbit holes in search of red threads now connects us. And, as Taylor Swift sings,

> "Isn't it just so pretty to think
> All along there was some
> Invisible string
> Tying you to me?"

CHAPTER 3

i'm all in

I'VE ALWAYS HAD AN INTEREST IN MINDFULNESS AND mental health. I don't remember where this interest came from or too many early experiences with mindfulness beyond my yoga classes. But I do remember the first time I meditated....

I was in a high school social studies class, and we were studying Eastern culture. Our teacher had us all lie down on the floor, close our eyes, and listen to him as he guided us through breathing and visualization. I remember when it was over, he asked how we felt, and I expressed how relaxed and calm I was...the most I've ever felt that way all through my high school career. He responded to me with a giant grin on his face and said, "I know! Isn't it amazing?"

I had no idea at the time how amazing meditation, mindfulness, and breathing would be for me in the future.

Fast forward to December of 2018. My friend and colleague, Rebecca, asked me if I wanted to join her at a workshop around mindfulness designed specifically for educators. She explained that I would learn some tools I could bring back to the classroom to help my students. We applied for the school department to fund our workshop, and we were off! This professional development, called "Breathe for Change," happened on a weekend, but we didn't mind. We were so excited to sit with like-minded educators and figure out how we could best show up and serve our students. Plus, it was a nice weekend away with a friend, so BONUS!

We not only had a GREAT time together but Rebecca and I learned a lot and met some really amazing people. In just two days, the bond between my colleague and me grew even stronger (I didn't think that was possible), and we connected on a deep level with the other educators at our workshop. While we were there, we learned about a bigger and much more intense training that we could attend in the near future that would certify us as yoga teachers, as well as give us a Social-Emotional Learning Facilitator certificate. In just the weekend alone, we learned so many things that we knew our colleagues and students could benefit from, and we were very excited at the possibility of learning more!

In March of 2019, I was off to Boston to start my official "Breathe for Change" training. This time, I was with another friend and colleague, Cara. And we were ready to attend this training every other weekend between March and May of that year. It was going to be a lot of work! But we felt excited at the possibilities of what was to come. We couldn't wait to gain more knowledge, learn more tools, and be ready for whatever our students need from us. Little did we know and understand that we would work on ourselves more than anyone else....

Breathe for Change taught me so much about myself. Throughout my training, I had a chance to tap into what it was like for me as a child and see what formed who I was as an adult. I had a chance to really look at why I had such an interest in mental health and wellness....I was honest with myself when I verbalized that I was into it because there was a personal connection there.

As a child, I had a good life! My favorite and most happy family memories were at the beach and on the boat, which is probably why

I continue to create those memories with my children today. I was an introspective child with a feeling of awe for the world - I always wanted to know why and learn more! I'm still that way, in fact. And just like I feel as an adult, as a child, I had a need to socialize, but I enjoyed a mix-in of solitude, as well. Writing was how I reflected on what was happening around me, and it became a huge passion of mine throughout my childhood. I enjoyed writing poetry, documenting my days in a journal, and making up stories that I wrote on stapled paper to resemble my first novels.

While I often lived on the pleasant side of the Mood Meter, as a kid, I felt most frustrated by injustices. I didn't like seeing kids bully each other. I hated arguments that happened between family members and often felt angry about them, even when they had nothing to do with me! I strayed very far from kids in school who treated others with disrespect and wanted nothing to do with them, which is why I think I struggled to fit into any one particular group of friends. I often had friends everywhere I went, only allowing those that I felt were kind and fair to get close to me.

This moral compass of mine made it difficult for me because I also had a desire to please everyone around me. I didn't want anyone to know I was upset or hurt by them. I thrived on positive reinforcement from adults in my life, especially my parents and teachers. I was the type of kid who did pretty much exactly what was expected of me, even if it wasn't always what I wanted to do. I wasn't super rebellious...just the normal kid/teenager stuff. I wasn't so unruly that I risked my well-being or the health of others around me. I didn't like to rock the boat. I hated it when I upset someone else. And I often apologized for things that I didn't really feel sorry for, only to please the other person that may have been upset with me. If I truly showed my anger or frustration to anyone or about anything, then I wouldn't be as perfect as I was trying to appear.

Breathe for Change helped me see that this "inner child" of mine came with me into adulthood. I started to see that my need to appear perfect was putting me in a pretty constant state of chronic stress. As an adult, I was still trying to be agreeable and often changing who I was to please others. Outside the occasional roommate or family member, I wouldn't often let myself be truly angry in public until I had kids. It was then that my children would push my buttons hard enough that all the anger I was trying to suppress exploded....and then I would feel embarrassed or worry about what others thought of me. I began to feel out of control, seeing that I wasn't allowing myself to be ME. I didn't even really know exactly who I was....

There was a day when my teachers at Breathe for Change invited me to think about what I wanted my life to be like after leaving this course....what did I want to do with my Yoga and SEL Facilitator certificates? That is where Calm Education was born....it didn't have that name, and it didn't look exactly like it does today. But the seed for my idea was planted. And it was the most authentic thing I could ever imagine doing in my career.

It has been five years since I graduated from Breathe for Change. When the course was over, I was craving more authenticity. It became harder to show up at work and please my colleagues and families, knowing that what I was doing with my students wasn't what I wanted. I needed more, and so did my students. I needed nourishment, and so did my own children. My inner intuitive kiddo stayed with me for a long time after I left Breathe for Change. She knew that I didn't have to stay where I was...that I could pursue my vision of teaching kids and working with families and educators on Social-Emotional tools and practices, which we all desperately need.

About three years after I left Breathe for Change, I decided to learn more about meditation. I learned a lot about it and was very clear on the benefits, so I was ready. Within a few short weeks, I learned how to meditate on my own twice a day. I took the course online but went to meet the teacher in person when COVID restrictions allowed me to travel to New York City. There, I met more like-minded people who were ready to make a change within themselves, as well. My regular meditation practice finally put me in a place where I was ready to make changes to my life so I could work toward my own healing and help others heal with me.

Through my meditation, the relationship I had with myself continued to change....I found more compassion for myself and others. And I was able to make difficult decisions about things with integrity. I started to realize that my own strength and power didn't depend as much on what the world thought of me.

These last five years have changed a lot for me. My interests in mindfulness and mental health brought me to learn and work on myself. My life turned in a direction where I saw a lot of suffering around me, and I was ready to be part of the change I wanted to see for the world. It took me a few years to finally make the decision to leave the public school classroom and pursue the idea that I concocted in my brain at my Breathe for Change class.

I've been in this role for almost two years now, and I try really hard to practice what I preach with my students, their families, and their teachers. I am, by no means perfect...which is why I use the word *practice*. I am a constant work in progress, which is something I try to tell my students every time I work with them. We are going to make mistakes along the way. But that's why it is important to surround ourselves with our incredible support systems. I depend on my close family and friends. I exercise. I get outdoors. I find guidance in counseling. I am working on my health and my sleep patterns.

And I breathe.

Society tells us to perform, out-perform, and compete. I feel like many people don't see the value in breathing. Why breathe when we can spend time reading, writing, and getting better grades? We need to start seeing the connection between mindfulness and success. It is important for us to show this to our children, too.

I'm not a doctor or a professional on the body, but I am pretty sure that breathing is the only involuntary function of the body that we can control! It is possible to use our breath to intervene when we are feeling something big! Teaching this to kids at a young age can make them more resilient and not so stuck in stress...always in a state of high alert, in a fearful mode, or in fight or flight. This is where the majority of our population is these days....

My experiences with mindfulness and mental health have taught me that emotion regulation is physical. We aren't taught how to do this. We need to learn! With self-awareness and wisdom, I am able to catch my negative thought cycles. I am much less reactive to the world than I used to be. I sleep better. And I feel safer.

I want the world to see that we all need guidance. We all want to be better people. We can all make mistakes, learn, continue, and shake it off. We need to understand that everything is in constant movement and that any big emotions that we feel are not definitive... they will pass with time and practice.

In my role as a Social-Emotional Learning Coach, I want to work towards building a community where everyone feels safe. My hope is that with baby steps, we can put an end to apathy and stop taking things for granted at home, in school, and in our work. If we can work towards teaching the next generation how to go inside themselves and how to connect as human beings, maybe together we can start to learn from each other and begin to break divisions.

And then everything really will be OK.

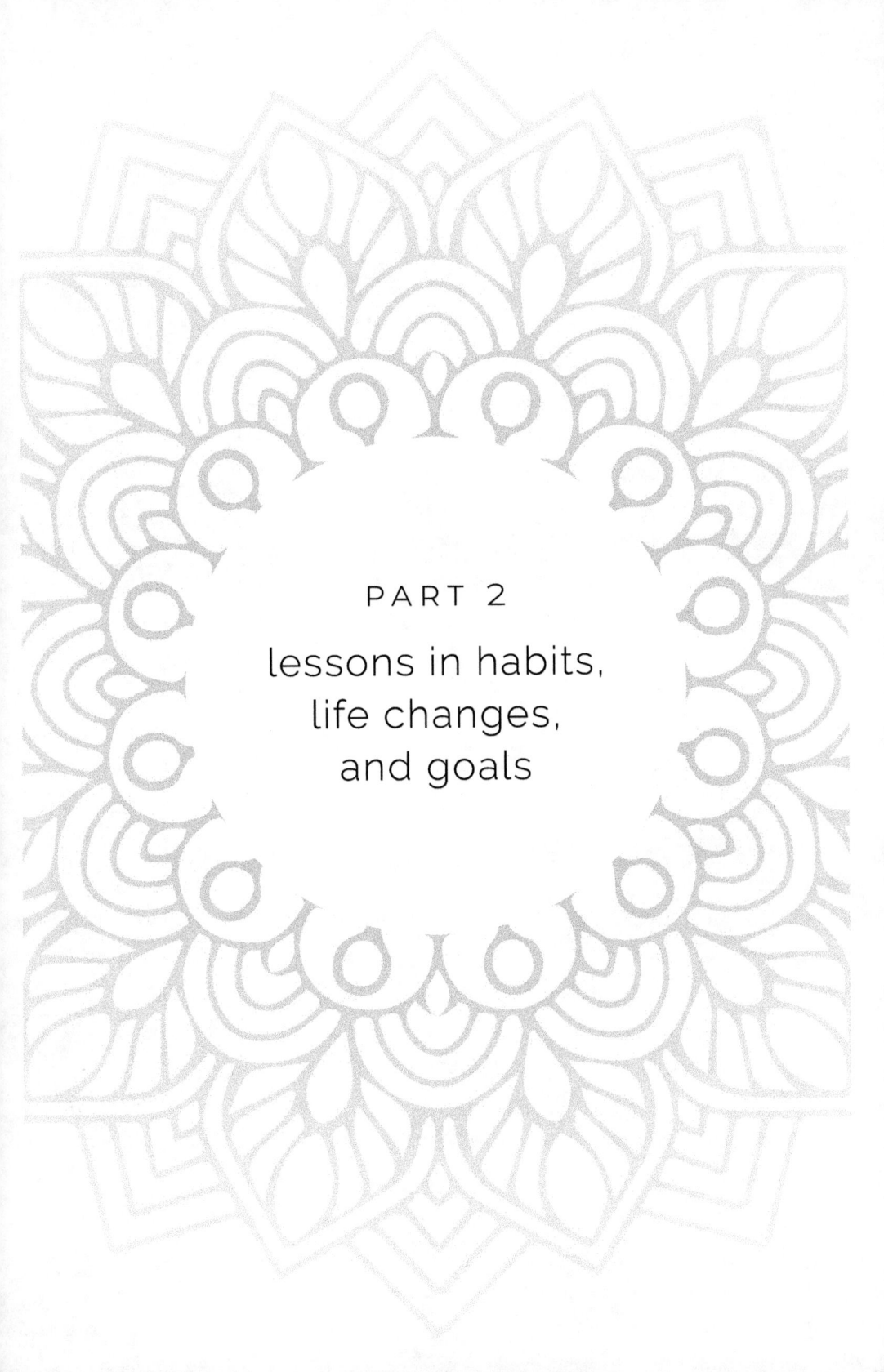

PART 2

lessons in habits,
life changes,
and goals

CHAPTER 4

a beginner's mind

ABOUT THREE YEARS AGO, I BEGAN A MEDITATION practice. I learned to meditate twice a day, on my own (without guidance), for twenty minutes at each sitting. This practice has opened up a world that I didn't realize existed. But more excitingly, it has connected me to a new group of friends.

For a few years now, every morning and every afternoon, when I am done meditating, I text a group of women with a short message to confirm I completed a sitting. These women are named Maggie, Catherine, Allison, and Lisa. Our text chain is called "Supermeditators," which I absolutely adore!

We met in New York City at Emily Fletcher's "Ziva Live" course. I had no idea how much this short weekend would impact my life. Since we left NYC, the five of us have become "accountability partners" for one another to help each other stick to our meditation practice. But there is more to our relationship than that. We also check in on each other regularly. It is through these check-ins that I receive the wisdom and ideas of these four amazing and smart women.

Their latest wisdom is the inspiration behind writing this particular story. A few days ago, over text, Catherine and Allison were lamenting about how challenging it can be to stick to this meditation practice. They shared that they had recently fallen out of regular practice but are getting back into it. Lisa, also a yoga instructor, shared her knowledge with us about something she called "a beginner's mind." I have heard this term in my yoga and meditation classes, so this wasn't the first time it piqued my curiosity. I decided to do some research that I want to share with you.

A beginner's mind is also referred to as "Shoshin." This is a term from Zen Buddhist teachings referring to the act of having an open mind, letting go of all preconceived notions, and looking at every aspect of life from a fresh and new perspective. It was brought to the West in the writings and speeches of the Japanese Zen Master, Shunryu Suzuki. He says,

> "In the beginner's mind, there are many possibilities. In the expert's mind, there are few."

In her text, Lisa reminded us about the practice of meditation. She shared her gratitude for finding this group of women. She pointed out the beauty in the fact that we give each other permission to keep coming back and beginning again in the meditation practice and with one another. That's when she mentioned what she knows about the beginner's mind. In her words, she explained that this means accepting what is and being open to what comes without self-judgment or expectation.

Suzuki suggests that having an open "beginner's" mind can have many benefits to our lives, such as fostering new skills, better decision-making, and greater empathy. **Dismissing expectations** is a vital practice of life!

Reading Lisa's text about the beginner's mind made me reflect on how I've been struggling against being a beginner my whole life! It sounds so easy to live in a world where we dismiss expectations and approach life with a beginner's mind. One major obstacle, however, is something called "confirmation bias." This is the human tendency to notice, focus on, and give credit to evidence that fits with our existing beliefs.

I will admit that I have an existing belief that I firmly stand by. Those of you who know me well can confirm that I believe that HARD WORK = SUCCESS. The friction in this existing belief occurs when I see a slump in my progress, and this has been happening my whole life.

As a kid in school, when I saw my grades drop, I would put in extra time studying and practicing my skills. Often, I would work to the point of exhaustion! I got good grades in school, but I never truly enjoyed being a student. I was so focused on the numbers that I didn't spend the time enjoying the new books I was reading or the new concepts I was learning.

When I got older, I decided I needed to focus on prioritizing my physical health, so I joined Weight Watchers. When I saw a slump in my weight loss, I would become really strict with myself, writing down everything that I ate and depriving myself of the things I enjoyed eating. Then I struggled to figure out why I could lose the weight but not keep it off.

As a teacher, I was very reliant on data about my students. I set goals for my students to achieve certain scores. In fact, many of our assessment programs projected future scores for students based on their previous growth. When I saw a drop in those scores or if a student didn't meet their projected goal, I would catch myself thinking, "I am not working hard enough." I would begin to hustle, working late to create interventions to help those students achieve. I lost sleep, getting caught up in ruminating thoughts about how my students' grades were a reflection of my effectiveness as a teacher.

There is no doubt that you have to put work into reaching your goals. I still believe that there is a link between working hard and success. But now I understand that when I didn't activate my beginner's mind when grades dropped, weight plateaued, or student scores stagnated, I lost the opportunity to look at all the *possibilities* behind these slumps in success. I became narrow-minded, working myself (and those around me) harder rather than smarter.

The key word in this realization about myself is POSSIBILITIES!!

There are so many possibilities in life, and I don't know about you, but I don't want to miss out on them! Without possibilities, the world would be very small. There wouldn't be new things to learn, new people to help you grow, new ideas to try out! It is kind of funny to think about it this way, but we are beginners in life—no one has done this before! As Lisa reminded me, the hard parts in life are there so we can grow, learn, and become stronger. Being a beginner can be scary, but it is also wildly exciting. Anything can happen!

So here I am, sitting here with a beginner's mind during this new phase of my teaching practice. Even though I have been an educator for over twenty years, this is a new realm for me, and I don't have the slightest idea what I am doing. And you know what? That's OK! It is *boring* to already have it figured out. There's nothing to achieve! It is such a relief that I don't have to be perfectly perfect all the time, always acting like I have it all together.

Just like my meditation, this is a practice....a lifelong practice. I'm on this journey like everyone else. I am relieved and happy to admit that I am multiple lifetimes away from being an expert at anything. I am thankful to say that I think this means my world won't be shrinking to a few possibilities anytime soon.

CHAPTER 5

this is me

AS DEFINED BY MERRIAM-WEBSTER, SELF-WORTH IS *A feeling that you are a good person who deserves to be treated with respect.* Self-worth involves how you act toward yourself and how you feel about yourself, especially compared to others.

I've had quite a few conversations about self-worth with both kids and adults in my world lately. So much so that I've noted things that have been said to me or even things I've thought about when it comes to my own self-worth and value. Some comments I've heard or thought are....

My social media followers are growing, and I'm so proud of myself!
I only have a few friends...not as many as other people.
I'm not a star player, so my role on the team isn't that important.
I am easily replaceable at work. If I leave, I don't think anyone will care.
I got an 89 on my history test. It's good, but it isn't an A.
I'm not making nearly as much money as last year.

I mean...I get it. I think it is part of the human experience to wonder where our place is in this world and how much we are truly valued by others. Our thoughts, feelings, and behaviors are closely tied to how we view our worthiness and value as human beings! I also think it is human nature to find self-acceptance through achievement and competition with others.

A lot of people have researched the impact that ability and effort have on our performance. I get the connection to these three things. And I also know that all three of those things—ability, effort, and performance—contribute to our feelings of worth and value. But when I listen to the thoughts of others in my life and the thoughts that go on in my own head, it makes me feel sad that we, as humans, put so much emphasis on our achievements. There is more to life that can contribute to our sense of self-worth than competing and "winning" against others.

I live in an affluent and highly competitive community. Our children's grades, the sports they play, the clubs we are part of, the cars we drive, what our houses look like, where we went to college…it all greatly matters, and it is something that many of us are well aware of! In fact, our local school department tries to combat the competitive nature of academics by not ranking students by their GPA and not celebrating valedictorians or salutatorians at high school graduation. Yet, kids as young as middle school (where their grades just begin to switch to averages from rubric scores) pay attention to their grade point average, wondering if what they are achieving is "good enough" and comparing their grades to others and ranking themselves in their minds.

The neighborhoods in our town are even ranked based on real estate value—the cost and size of houses, the proximity to the water, and the average income of the families living there. The neighborhoods and the town, compared to others in the state, also rank their schools. In turn, this sometimes both helps and hurts the real estate market. Our town prides itself on being number one academically in the state. As a result, our housing costs are high (even though they are high everywhere at the moment)! Where our kids go to college, especially compared to other towns and neighborhoods, matters! And even though our school system tries to combat it, we are all well aware that our students' grades and test scores matter, too.

The town I live in determines its self-worth based on school rankings, test scores, housing prices, income, and business offerings—everything that determines value as far as effort, abilities, and performance go.

But all of this is human nature, right?

The number on the scale.

The size of our clothes.

The brand of clothes we wear.

Our income.

The location of our home.

The car we drive.

The people we associate with.

What we do for a career.

The sport we play.

The college we attend.

Our amount of social media followers.

Do these things **really** make *me* more or less worthy? These thoughts swim in my mind all the time....

This makes me go back to that dictionary definition of what self-worth really is...*feeling like I am a good person who deserves respect.*

Whether I wear expensive, affordable, or repurposed clothes...

Whether I am a teacher, a lawyer, or I work at a superstore...

Whether I have 20 followers or 20,000 followers on social media...

Whether I am young or old...

How much money I make...

Whether I am married, divorced, or single...

Whether I wear black or bright colors...

Whether I choose to go to college...

In other words, the things that make me feel happy (even if they aren't widely accepted or are "sophisticated" enough) *shouldn't* determine how much respect I deserve or how much respect I give myself. The point is, we are all human! **Humans want and deserve to be respected and accepted!**

Here is where we get to the heart of the matter—as humans, we are the only ones that determine our SELF-worth. That is why the word "self" is in there. Even if we don't believe we are worthy and valuable (or that someone else is)...guess what?! We are! It is important to switch the narrative we say out loud and in our heads about our worthiness and the worthiness of others.

Writing my thoughts about this reminds me of a time in my teaching career when I would get very worked up about teacher evaluations. Every few years, I needed to participate in an evaluation cycle where my principal would observe a few lessons and rate my performance based on a rubric. I also set math and reading goals for my students and used measurable data to determine whether my students met, didn't meet, or exceeded the goals I set for them. I would do the same for myself by setting "professional growth goals." Plus, I rated myself, and my principal rated me on professional responsibilities set out by the state. All of those items would combine to create a score to determine whether I was highly effective, effective, developing, or ineffective as an educator.

Every year that I participated, I scored as effective.

And that wasn't good enough for me.

I was often left feeling frustrated, sad, and disappointed that I wasn't ranked "highly effective." Some of my colleagues were rated that way, and I felt like I was just as good as them at teaching. I couldn't wrap my head around it, and I always felt that I was never going to be "good enough."

Stop and think about that for a second....

I was ranked effective! ***Darn straight, I was an effective public school teacher!***

My students loved me, and I saw them grow as humans and learners every single year! I got amazing feedback from parents. Countless kids told me that I was their "favorite teacher" (and still do!). I thrived in front of a classroom full of kids. I love to teach!

And that is more than enough for me.

See how I flipped that narrative right there?

As an educator, I have a variety of abilities and talents. As a public school teacher, I got a wide range of results from my efforts depending on the class that was sitting in front of me. But no matter what the teacher evaluation tool told me, I understood that the score I was given was how I performed and how my students performed, which is something I can't really control! It wasn't a measure to determine who I am or how good of a teacher I am. It didn't matter that I didn't win any educator awards or get a "highly effective" rating on my evaluation.

I know that I am a good person.

I know that I was a good public school teacher who greatly cared for and loved my students.

And I know that, no matter what, I deserve respect...from myself and others.

It took me a while to see this and really feel it. But it is so important that we model this for our young people and help them understand and accept their own self-worth. We need to reinforce their **value as BEING a human.** Isn't that why we are called human "beings" rather than human "doings?"

If we show the young people in our lives that we love and appreciate them for exactly who they are, they will learn that it's ok to love themselves for exactly who they are. Kids don't need to *achieve* anything to earn our love and respect.

As for ourselves as adults? That's a bit trickier...how do we increase our own self-worth? Modeling this for our kids is so important! I guess I need to constantly remind myself that my self-worth isn't determined by material things—including social media, the way I look, my job title, my income, or my score on an evaluation.

It is so easy to get caught up in that stuff, especially living in a time when these things are valued by society in general. I truly need to make efforts to take steps back and think about what truly matters in determining my own worth (and the worth of others around me!).

I also need to work on that critical inner voice. I need to identify it, challenge it, and continue to externalize it so that I can manage the nitpicking and flaw counting that my inner voice likes to do sometimes. If I let her win too often, she will begin to think she is right, and I don't have time for that!!

A good friend of mine used to remind me to think about what I would like written on my headstone when I die. I know that sounds morbid, but she was right!

Do I want my headstone to read....

She scored as "highly effective" on her teacher evaluations and drove a nice car. She was very fashionable with a trim waist and designer shoes.

Or would I rather people remember me as....

She was a kind and loving wife, daughter, mother, and friend. She was thoughtful, empathetic, and a good listener.

What would you guess is most valuable to measuring my self-worth? I think you know the answer....

I know my friend's reminder to think about what I want others to say about me when I leave this world is a little dark. But I think what she was trying to tell me is exactly what was said by Ernest T. Cambell back in the 1970s (Fun Fact: some think it was Mark Twain who said this, but this has been contested....):

The two most important days in your life are the day you are born and the day you find out why.

...a good reminder that feeling worthy and valuable has absolutely nothing to do with effort, achievement, and the competitive nature of human beings.

It is simply that ***you are you,*** and ***that is always going to be enough.***

CHAPTER 6

crafting your order

I LOVE TO GO OUT TO EAT! I PARTICULARLY LOVE EATING out at a new restaurant I've never been to before. I'll go online and check out what the restaurant has to offer, dreaming and planning what meal I'd like to have. Knowing what I am going to eat ahead of time takes the pressure off having to peruse the menu while socializing with my friends or family. I can simply order, relax, and enjoy the food and the company! The whole restaurant experience completely entices the foodie inside of me!!

Why am I telling you this? Because I would like to use my thoughts about going out to eat and looking at the menu ahead of time as a metaphor for *manifesting.*

Manifesting is a mainstream buzzword of the moment. I hear people use it all the time! For example, a group of friends and I were out together the other night. One of my friends expressed her frustrations at work, described how things could be better, and shared what her dream job would look like. Another friend, listening to all of this, responded with, "You can find that dream job! Just manifest it!"

I wish it worked that way...that would be pure magic.

So what exactly is manifesting, and how does it work? Some people describe it as a practice of thinking positive thoughts with the purpose of making those thoughts a reality. In all honesty, this description can make manifesting sound pretty hokey. We can't "just manifest" something into reality. That sounds more like wishing than manifesting to me. And there is a distinct difference between the two, which I'll try to explain in a second.

But first, let me go back to my restaurant analogy. When we go to a restaurant and place an order for our meal, we tell the waitstaff exactly what we want, how we like it cooked, what we'd like on the side, and more. Then, a little while later, it all appears in front of us so we can enjoy what we asked for!

Imagine for a second that the waiter comes to my table to take my order, and I tell them that I don't know what I want and to simply "surprise me." Or maybe I give them a list of a few things I'd maybe enjoy but give them permission to pick something for me. Imagine that I am the most undecided restaurant patron on the planet!

What will the waiter bring me? It is possible they will bring me something that I like but don't particularly enjoy and relish. Or, they may bring me something that I totally dislike, ruining my restaurant experience! The possibilities of what actually lands on the plate in front of me are totally unknown.

Manifesting is kinda like that...you have to be clear in what you want to create.

I like to try new restaurants because I have a passion for food. I want to treat myself because I know I deserve it! I don't want to pay for a meal that I will regret. I know what I want to eat and exactly what menu item ignites something inside of me.

I manifest because I have a passion for something. I want this something because it gives me purpose and meaning, and I know that I am worthy. I don't want to live a life that I will regret. I know what I want in my life and exactly what will ignite something inside of me.

See the connection?

Wait...there's more....

My excitement for restaurants goes beyond my passion for food. Going to a restaurant in hopes that I will eat the meal of my dreams is simply wishful thinking. It is important for me to take action to ensure I will enjoy my meal. I look at the menu ahead of time. When I get to the restaurant, I ask my friends or family what they are ordering and take stock of if I am ordering the best meal that I can! I sometimes even ask the waiter for their opinion on my meal choice. I look around to see what other tables have ordered and what might seem enticing to me.

Right here is the difference between wishing and manifesting....

Wishing is simply saying something that you want and hoping magic will bring it to you. Sometimes this works, and sometimes it doesn't, right?

Manifesting starts with a wish *but then takes action.*

I start with hopes about something I want in my life, and then I take action to nurture this dream into reality. Maybe I use affirmations or positive visualizations in my meditations or before I fall asleep at night. From there, I do my research by looking at other people who have already achieved this dream. Then, I take my first step toward my manifestation. From there, any actions I take toward my dream get easier and easier and eventually come into reality.

Manifestation makes a claim on what I want, and then I act accordingly.

Just like the restaurant...I make a claim on the meal I would like, and then I place the order exactly the way I would like it to be served to me.

Manifesting can be challenging if you don't embody what you'd like to create, however. Embodiment is the difference between a real-life amazing meal at a restaurant and a simple drawing of the meal.

Visualizing what I want in my mind isn't enough. I also need to figure out how to move past my limiting beliefs...to work through the fears I might have about how deserving I am. Manifesting doesn't work if it comes from a place of judgment.

Let me give you a real-life example...my fitness journey seems like the easiest place to start.

For years, I wished for a better body. One that didn't have stretch marks or wobbly bits. One that had muscle tone and a flat belly. I visualized this dream body before I went to bed at night. I thought positively that *someday I would lose weight and live in a body that I loved.*

I took action. I went on diets. I exercised more. I weighed myself. I went to Weight Watcher meetings, and I lost weight.

...but I never kept the weight off, and I never had my "dream" body.

It wasn't until recently that I realized I was manifesting things all wrong. How was that possible?? I had a wish! I was visualizing it! I was taking action!

I was forgetting one important part...

Belief.

Belief in myself.

Belief that I was deserving.

I had this wish of a "dream body" because I judged every ounce of the body that I was gifted. I looked at all my imperfections and formed negative opinions about every single one of my physical flaws. I was manifesting a better body because I hated the one that I was walking around in!

How could I manifest my dream when I wasn't being clear about what I wanted?

I didn't want a better body!

I wanted a new one.

And that isn't humanly possible. I was trying to place a blind order with the universe that was bound to leave me grossly unsatisfied...just like placing a wishy-washy order at a restaurant!

It is taking me some time, but I am slowly starting to appreciate the body that I have been given. My body is alive. My body created and delivered two amazing children. My body is a complex and incredible machine.

Once I began to lose the harsh judgment towards myself, what I wanted to manifest became clearer.

I wanted to be healthy and fit.

And that is a very clear order to place for my manifestation.

My meditation teacher, Emily Fletcher, was on to something when she told me that manifesting is like "placing an order with the cosmic waitress." Manifesting takes a dream, mixes it with faith and belief in oneself, includes actions toward those beliefs, and then delivers.

Without fear.

And that's the essence of manifesting—placing a clear order with the universe, just like ordering from a menu at a new restaurant. As you navigate your own manifestations, remember to be clear about what you truly desire, believe in your worthiness to receive it, and take purposeful actions toward your dreams.

It is about embodying your desires, banishing self-doubt, and a willingness to embrace the process. Once that happens, the universe has a way of delivering exactly what you need.

Pure magic.

CHAPTER 7

the problem with my habits

FOR THE LAST SIX MONTHS OR SO, I'VE BEEN REALLY trying hard to focus on my health. I have started to workout daily and have included weightlifting in my routine. I have started to track what I eat every day, monitoring my calories consumed and increasing my protein and fiber intake. But in the last few months, I've noticed an increase in my weight, and I don't like it. So, I decided to take a close look at the things that I do every day and ask myself why I do these things.

I have a book recommendation for you that is a great one to read, especially with the start of the New Year and the creation of resolutions. I read this book while I was tutoring a college student. She needed help with her executive functioning skills, so we decided to do a mini book club with *Atomic Habits* by James Clear. The author proposes "easy and proven ways to build good habits and break bad ones." It is a straightforward read with lots of great stories and anecdotes that kept me interested throughout my reading. One thing that really resonated with me that James Clear writes in his book is,

" Your outcomes are a lagging measure of your habits. Your net worth is a lagging measure of your financial habits. Your weight is a lagging measure of your eating habits...you get what you repeat."

So yeah...wow...James is pretty clear (no pun intended...or maybe it was). My increasing weight is the measure of my eating habits. I am getting what I am repeating. That's why I wanted to take a look at what habits I have gotten into lately that are giving me these results. I decided to make a list of what I've been doing and why I do these things. Here's what I discovered:

HABIT #1: *I get up early, before the rest of my family, to exercise every day.* I do this because I know I won't have the motivation to do my workout later in the day. Getting up to do my workouts gives me a purpose and ensures my exercise will get done.

HABIT #2: *I write down what I eat and drink for breakfast, lunch, dinner, and snacks.* I do this because I know it will help me count calories and increase/monitor my protein and fiber intake.

HABIT #3: *I pre-plan what I am going to eat every day as best as I can.* I do this so I can be sure I am staying on track and keeping myself focused. If I know what I'm planning to eat ahead of time, I won't stray from my menu, eating something I didn't plan for...

HABIT #4: *A few times a week, I eat a few Club Crackers with Nutella and don't track it.* I'm not sure why I do this. I probably do it because I am bored. And I really, really, really love Nutella combined with the crunch of the cracker. I can be a sweet-aholic.

HABIT #5: *I don't always accurately weigh and measure my food when*

I prepare it...sometimes, I just "eyeball" it. I do this because I am in a rush and simply don't feel like measuring. I am probably becoming complacent about something I was doing at the beginning of this journey that was helpful.

HABIT #6: *I drink 108oz of water every day.* I do this because I know water intake helps with weight loss. It is also good for my skin. I feel better when I hydrate.

HABIT #7: *Most weeks, I only drink alcohol on the weekend.* I do this because alcohol has too many calories, and I'd rather eat my calories than drink them! I also sleep better when I don't have alcohol in my system.

HABIT #8: *Sometimes, I only write down that I had one glass of wine when really I had more than that....and I don't measure the size of my glass.* I do this because I've been depriving myself. I know I want two glasses of wine, but I don't save myself enough calories when I pre-plan. I don't save myself enough calories because I tell myself I'd rather eat my calories, but once I get a glass of wine in me, I also want another one of those....

OK....so don't judge me over these habits. As I began to truly think about my habits, write them down, and reflect on why I do these things, I know why I am gaining weight.

The bad habits are crystal clear on this list. However, James Clear would tell me that there are no "good" or "bad" habits....there are only effective habits. All habits serve me in some way, even the "bad" ones, which is why I repeat them. Instead of thinking about good or bad habits, I should really look at the things that I do and decide if they will net me positive or negative outcomes. Not weighing my food, avoiding tracking because I am over my calories, and sneaking

Nutella and Club Crackers will make me gain weight. This is not an outcome I want to continue.

All this thinking about my health goals and habits got me thinking about other habits I have in my life. How can I improve my financial situation? How can I keep my house in better order? How can I be more organized? What habits have I formed that influence these things?

This is why I am writing about this topic in my story. I am hoping that I can inspire you to do the same.

What habits do you perform that net positive outcomes?

And, what habits net negative outcomes?

Is there anything that is making you wonder why things aren't going the way you want them to?

If you are feeling this, I encourage you to write a list of your habits and whys, as well. Once you know the habits you want to change, the work can begin.

I guess I have a project ahead of me. It is time to break out my *Atomic Habits* book and re-read the chapters about the steps I can take to change the habits that aren't serving me on my weight loss journey. One thing I know for sure is that I truly believe that I am a fit person. If I think and believe this, that is what I will become. So, on that note, I think I'll begin by going through my cabinets…time to chuck the Nutella! Takers, anyone?

CHAPTER 8

not everything you love is good for you

WE HEAR IT ALL THE TIME FROM SELF-CARE WEBSITES, articles, and social media....

Do what you love. Love what you do.

Do what makes you happy.

Whatever you decide to do, be sure it brings you joy.

Enjoy the present rather than being anxious about what the future holds.

Being happy never goes out of style.

Life is too short to do anything other than what brings you pleasure.

Live life as if you'll die today.

This week, I discovered that this is the **worst** advice anyone could ever give you. Let me explain....

I love the summer. I love the beach and the boat. I love the ocean waves and the sunshine. My happiest days are spent in the summer sun. I jokingly say that I am solar-powered. As a teacher, if I didn't have my summer vacations full of sun and fun, I don't know what I would have done to survive. As a parent, bringing my kids outside for fresh air in the summer kept them calmer during the witching hours of the late afternoon and evening. Summer sunshine is heaven to me.

Being by the water brings me back to my childhood. I remember spending morning to late afternoon at the beach with my mom, my sister, and our neighbor's family. We'd eat peaches, peanut butter sandwiches, and all sorts of treats while sitting on our beach towels. I would spend so much time in the water that my lips would wrinkle from being waterlogged. When we got home, my sister and I would shower with our green garden hose in the backyard, and then we would spend the last few hours of sunlight while my parents made dinner, "painting" the house with a bucket of water and a brush. Getting into bed after a day like this felt amazing. To this day, I sleep better after an afternoon with my feet in the sand than on any other given day.

I also remember days out on the boat. Sometimes, my parents would let me invite a friend, and we would set sail sitting on the bow of the boat together, letting our feet hang over the edge, hoping for a wave to splash our toes. My mom would say she was going down below to read, but we would joke that she was reading the back of her eyelids because we knew perfectly well that she was taking a nap. The boat was the place where our family could let it all go, relax, and enjoy the salt air and the feeling of the sun on our shoulders.

I have very olive-colored skin. And in the summer, my skin is like a beacon flashing, and I am quite the sun worshipper. One time, my husband and I went to Florida, and one of his southern friends declared, "My! She is as brown as a berry!" (cue southern accent). I have always been proud of my tan lines. And I think many women would agree that our "wobbly bits" (borrowed from Bridget Jones) look way better sunkissed than they do in the winter.

As a kid, I never did anything to protect my skin from the sun. We didn't have to! No one told us about the dangers. But as I got older, my dermatologists warned me, time and time again, to protect myself. Wear a hat, stay under an umbrella, and reapply sunscreen. Whelp….two out of three ain't bad. I am pretty religious with my sunscreen. But a hat is hot, and the umbrella shields me from being able to truly sun worship, so that wasn't happening.

Until today.

Yup.

You heard me.

Today, I am going to the dermatologist to have a large portion of the skin on the back of my leg taken off. I will have a good amount of stitches, too. I was diagnosed with Melanoma. My sister was diagnosed a few years ago. My mom was diagnosed recently, as well. Is this hereditary? Or is it environmental? Who knows…but if I continue on my sun-worshipping path, I know it won't be good for me. So, if I can cut out the environmental risks, that's half the battle, right?

I went for my bi-annual appointment with the skin doctor last week. I go twice a year because of my family history and the amount of moles that I genetically have. I, once again, listened to the lecture. My doctor told me that I have more tan lines than any other patient in his practice and that I need to stay out of the sun. As always, I listened and nodded. But there was no way he was going to take the sun away from me…or at least I thought. As he reviewed my moles, he noticed one on the back of my right leg, just behind my knee and near my inner thigh. He was hesitant and almost decided to leave it and see what it looked like in six months. But then, at the last minute, he decided to give it a little scrape and test it. The results would be back in two weeks…call him if I didn't hear from him…he really didn't think it was anything.

About four days later, he called me personally. "You have Melanoma," he said.

I have Melanoma.

Thankfully, my doctor has a good eye. Thankfully, he decided to remove it. And thankfully, it is simply at Stage 0...in the top layer of skin. Nothing else needs to be done. He will remove it, and it will be gone. I will be OK, and I will be forever grateful for this doctor, his talent, and his attention to detail.

But I'll still have the scar.

And I won't have the sun.

I texted a few friends about it, two of which are my running buddies. I won't be able to run with stitches for a few weeks, so I wanted to give them a heads-up. "Big hats and umbrellas will be our new style," they shared. "You know we love that look."

So I guess I'm going to dust off the umbrella I bought my husband to take to the beach, which is sitting in the garage somewhere. And I guess I'm in the market for a new hat. Something stylish... should I go with Julia Robert's style in the movie *Pretty Woman*? Or maybe something a little more cowgirl-ish? Sporty? My friend Katie always wore a cute straw hat with a giant red ribbon around it, and I thought she looked amazing. When I see someone wearing something like it, I always think of her and smile. Maybe I'll find something to match her style....

Either way, I know I can still find my recharge by the sea. I just have to do it a little differently than I have in the past. It's not just the sun that does it for me. It is also the salt water, the fresh air, the sand, and the loved ones that share it with me.

But as far as the advice that self-help columns and websites like to share with us, I am going to add something to these tidbits of information to make them a little more worthwhile. Here goes....

Do what you love and love what you do, *as long as it is a healthy choice*.

Do what makes you happy, *as long as it is good for you*.

Whatever you decide to do, be sure it brings you joy *and that you are still protecting yourself.*

Enjoy the present rather than being anxious about what the future holds, *but know that the choices you make can greatly affect what's in store for you.*

Life is too short to do anything other than what brings you pleasure, so do it, *but rethink it so that you can continue to live for as long as life will have you.*

Live as if you want to keep living for as long as you can!

We all have our vices…I've known for a long time that the sunshine on my shoulders makes me happy, but it wasn't a healthy choice. This whole experience has made me re-examine what else I may do in life that isn't always the healthiest choice I can make…Is it the way I eat? What I choose to do for exercise? The relationships I keep? I share this in hopes that you'll do the same…. Sometimes, what you think makes you happy isn't really going to do the trick in the long run.

Composer and theater director Richard Wagner had it right when he said:

"Joy is not in things. It is in us."

Summertime is *my* time. It is when I feel my best. I am relaxed. Time goes on forever. The sun and salt water nourish me. And I don't just "do" summer to make me happy…I relish in it. I frolic in it. I lounge in it. It is my heaven on Earth. But I've learned that my joy isn't really in the sun or my tan lines. Joy is inside of me because of what summer has meant to me my whole life. No amount of Melanoma will ever change that, right?

My lesson? Being happy never goes out of style, and neither do hats, apparently.

What "style" will you bring to your happiness so that you are able to do what makes you happy *and* take care of your well-being at the same time? Think about it….

CHAPTER 9

there's a gift in gray chin hairs

ON OCTOBER 5TH, 2023, I TURNED FORTY-SIX.

A lot of people in their forties and beyond that I talk to don't want to celebrate their birthdays. Me? Of course, I want to celebrate!

In all honesty, I'll celebrate anything. I'll celebrate getting out the door on time on a Monday morning. I'll celebrate the C that one of my kids worked their tails off to earn in their hardest class. I'll most certainly celebrate any occasion with anyone, and I'll always find a good reason.

I think most people my age don't want to celebrate getting older. It is funny how that shifts from when we were kids. We couldn't wait to get older and hit the milestones....thirteen, sweet sixteen, eighteen, twenty-one!

Do you remember what age you stopped counting?

Maybe most of us stop counting around age thirty. I can speak for myself when I say that milestone made me feel really nervous to approach. It's the age when society tells us we are adults and we should be married, have kids, have a good-paying job...and if we don't add up, that age can be scary to reach. It is also a milestone where we feel we should "have it all together." But let me ask you, at what point in our lives do we *really* have it all together? Those of you that are older than me, please tell me! Because I haven't found that age yet.

Over lunch, talking about age, one of my friends told me that they stopped counting how old they were after forty. **They stopped counting?** Why? How? Does stopping the count take away the fact that we are aging? I think that it just puts us in denial.

I mean…let's think about it for a second. The minute we are born, we are getting older. Let that sink in. We've been going through life getting older **this whole time!**

And so much has happened! I've made it this far….

I made it through infancy and into toddlerhood, learning how to walk and talk (not an easy feat!).

I made it through adolescence and puberty (thank goodness we can't go backward in age!!).

I made it through bad breakups.

I made it through heartache.

I made it through miscarriages.

I made it through grief.

Each year that has passed has left me with scars, wrinkles, and gray hairs. Proof that I am getting older, yes. But also proof that **I am living**.

I'm living with my two amazing children, who have so much to give this world.

I'm living through the eyes of my funny and loving niece.

I'm living with the love and support of my awesome (and handsome) husband.

I'm living through a career change and the start of something new.

I'm living through the change of seasons from bathing suits to sweater weather.

I'm living through all the ups and downs that life offers me on a daily.

Last year, two friends of mine were taken from this world way too soon. It was a reminder of how quickly things can change and how truly amazing it is that I am chosen to continue to walk this Earth. I feel like I have so much left to see and do in this world. I have so much more to make it through...to *live* through. How lucky am I??

I spent some time this morning Googling quotes about aging. I invite you to read and take a pause on this one for a second:

> "If you're not getting older, you're dead."
> —Tom Petty

Oooof...that's a direct and to-the-point message! But what I think he's trying to say is:

Getting older is a privilege of living.

Getting older is something not everyone gets to do.

Celebrating a birthday is about celebrating something we've been doing since we were born...aging...making it through...***living.***

I found another quote in my Google Search this morning. I just couldn't help myself. There's a lot of good wisdom out there about getting older. This one is by one of my favorite authors from my childhood. She says:

> "The great thing about getting older is that you don't lose all the ages you've been."
> —Madeleine L'Engle

At one point, I used to relish hitting the "benchmark" ages.

I loved being thirteen! That's when I had my first kiss.

And eighteen? That's when I met my husband!

At age twenty-one? Sorry, Mom and Dad...that wasn't the age of my first drink, but it sure was a fun birthday celebration!

I had my first "real" teaching job by age twenty-two.

I was married at age twenty-seven.

I had my son at thirty-one and my daughter at thirty-five.

Today, at age forty-six, I'm not losing any of that! **All those ages that I've been have brought me to where I am now.** And there isn't anywhere else I'd rather be.

A few weeks ago, I went to get my eyebrows waxed and shaped. It is something I do regularly; no judgment, please! If you knew me when I was in my younger years, you would have seen the caterpillars that passed as eyebrows on my face. Although a good friend of mine pointed out the resemblance between my eyebrows and those of Brooke Shields back in her younger years, so I am going to run with that....

Anyway, while I was there, the woman giving me the wax pointed out a few hairs on my chin. She asked if she could remove those, too. Wait...what? Chin hairs? *Gray chin hairs?*

"Please," I told her. "Get rid of those quickly."

I'm not a fan of the signs I have of aging. I know the gray chin hairs are just the beginning of what's to come. I honestly don't even want to think about it. Instead, I am going to choose to think about what I can do to keep myself young. Just because I am getting older doesn't mean I have to get old.

Did you know we all have a fountain of youth inside of us? In my search for quotes, I came across another great one by Sophia Loren. She says,

> "There is a fountain of youth: it is your mind, your talents, the creativity you bring to your life and the lives

of people you love. When you learn to tap this source, you will truly have defeated age."

Thank you for that one, Sophia. I needed that today. I needed to be reminded that there is so much more to me than the number forty-six and my gray chin hairs.

I am writing this today to remind myself, on my forty-sixth birthday and beyond, that I am living. I have so much to offer this world and so many great things in my future to receive. There are people that love me, and I love in return. And I am tapping into all of it, no matter how much heartbreak I feel. No matter my struggles or my grief. No matter if I have gray chin hairs.

Next time you feel that achy back, find that stray hair where it doesn't belong, or notice something unpleasant about your age, remember this.

You are more than your age.

You are more than the number of years you have walked this Earth.

Your age has brought you to where you are now.

And it is a good place to be.

What's my plan for the next forty-six years? I'm going to take Sophia's advice and tap into the sources of creativity and love that I have around me. I'm going to take it and be amazing!

Who's with me??

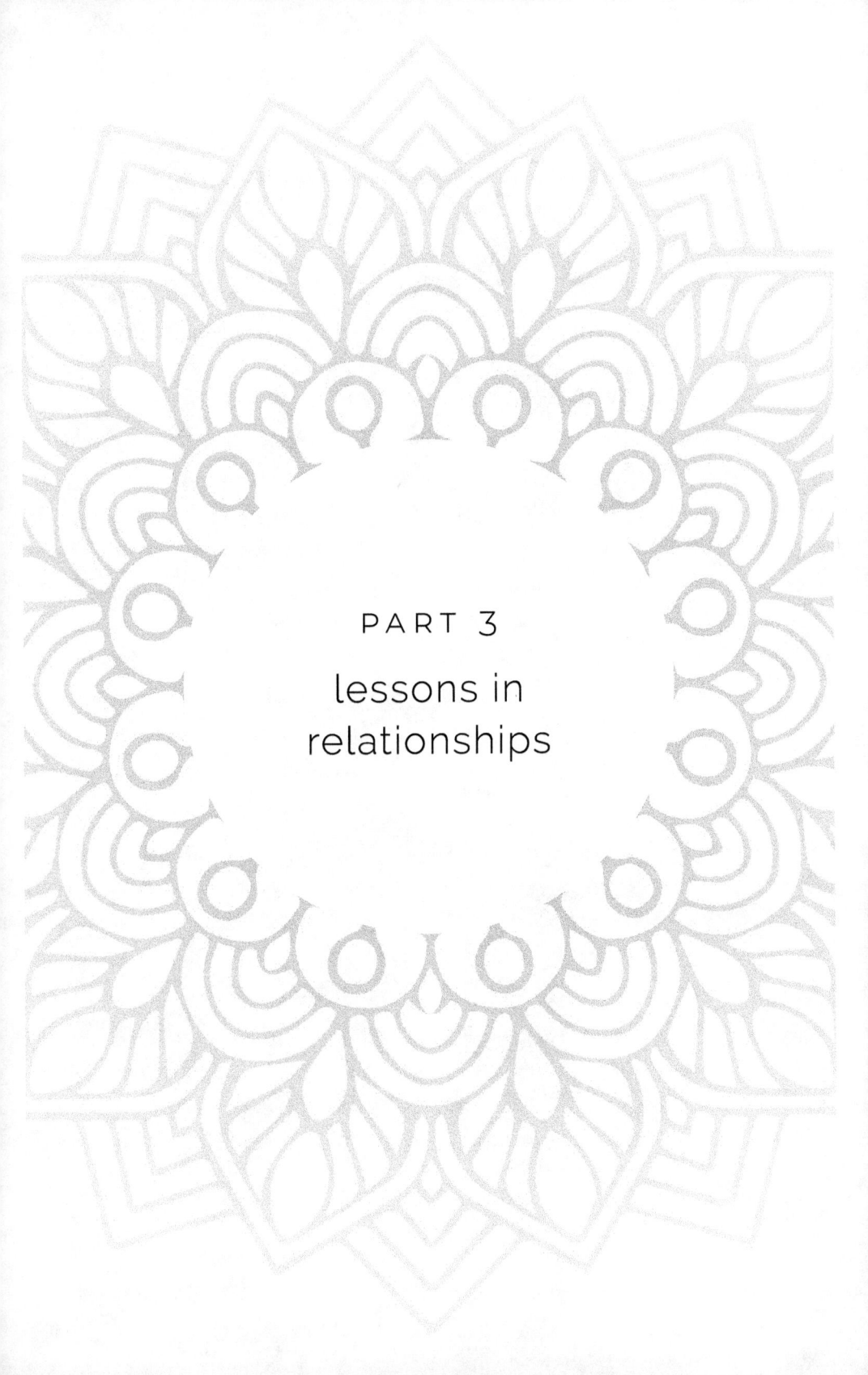

PART 3

lessons in relationships

CHAPTER 10

what do you know

WHAT DO WE KNOW ABOUT THE PEOPLE THAT WE SURround ourselves with? Our friends, our co-workers, our acquaintances that share our interests, parents of our child's friends, even a few family members....

I bet we know their likes and dislikes. We understand their personality. We might know a bit about their cultural heritage. We know about their family. We know what they do for a job. We probably even know a secret or two about them...something that they don't usually share with the entire world.

But do we *really* know them? Do we know....

about the things that weigh them down?
how they might respond to certain conflicts?
their approaches to relationships and raising a family?
what makes them feel secure?
their beliefs and attitudes about the world?
their biggest fears?
what they truly need?

their self-concept?
their traumatic experiences?

I remember learning about "The Iceberg Model" in a few of the classes and trainings that I've attended. This uses the iceberg as a metaphor for why people do what they do or how much we really know and understand about others. It is said that when looking at an iceberg, you can really only see about ten percent of it above the surface of the water. The other ninety percent of the iceberg is below the surface, hidden from view.

So, how are humans like icebergs?

Humans and icebergs can both float.
Both are made mostly of water.
For both people and icebergs, you can only see a little bit of them.
Most of an iceberg or a person you can't see.

Only about ten percent of what makes us who we are and what shapes our behavior is floating above the surface for all to see—the tip of the iceberg. The other ninety percent of us isn't so easily revealed but has a great influence on our behavior and decision-making—the part of the iceberg that sits below the surface.

What we know about the people we choose to surround ourselves with is really just the tip of the iceberg. In other words, sometimes what we see in people is what they want us to see or what is obvious to us.

What parts of people are considered "above the surface?" We can learn a lot by looking at a person without spending very much time with them—their gender, age range, race, and the language they speak. But even then, some of these things that we **think** we can see can't always be understood just by looking at a person. Realistically, the only things we know about someone are the things they are comfortable sharing with us and the rest of the world.

Alternatively, it can be problematic to think we know someone based on the surface level. We can create inaccurate assumptions, stereotypes, or "othering" of people who appear different from ourselves. To avoid this, we need to dive below the surface. But to get someone to open up and trust you, it is important to display genuine curiosity, patience, an open heart...

And compassion.

The things about others that can't be seen above the waterline are parts of their identity that take more time to learn or may only be revealed to certain people. These things can include family structures, worries, health challenges, learning differences...the deeper aspects of ourselves.

And without compassionate humans, these things will never be revealed if we don't feel safe.

At a meeting this week, we discussed this very issue. We were talking about what it means to be "trauma-informed." As educators and those working with children and families, it is important to understand that everyone has something they are "dealing with." If we approach everyone, understanding that they may be experiencing or have experienced some level of trauma, then we are able to work with them in a more compassionate way, with a bigger understanding of them as humans.

For example, if we are in a store and we see someone yelling at an employee—like really going off the handle—we may think to ourselves, "Wow! What is wrong with that person?"

But if we look at the situation with curiosity, patience, and an open heart at what is below the surface, we may instead think to ourselves, "Wow! What happened to that person to make them respond that way?"

There's that compassion.

It is a very simple mind shift.

And it is exactly that change in thinking that will create understanding and genuine care for not only the people that we choose to surround ourselves with but *all* humans. As Anne Frank wrote,

"No one has ever become poor by giving."

Our world would see so much abundance if we all tried to understand that there is a lot more to each other than we can see and are willing to share with others. We could be rich with...

Love
Patience
Consideration
Tolerance
Empathy
...maybe even enlightenment!

And while we are one of billions of people, this connectedness and compassion will help us as individuals to know we are not alone. That our friends, family, and everyone in this world are simply trying to be humans together...
...and be the best version of ourselves that we can be.

CHAPTER 11

we are all connected

MY MEDITATION TEACHER IS ALWAYS SAYING AND reminding me that,

> "There is only one thing, and we are all it."

But what does that mean exactly?
I am not a tree.
I am not the animal that lives in a tree.
I am not anything but me.

In fact, science tells me that I am a unique combination of cells and DNA that no one else can replicate. How can I be what everyone else is?

This week, I think I realized what my meditation teacher was saying to me. WARNING: I go a little deep here...

Have you ever seen or studied a mandala? We often see them in yoga studios or other places where people may practice mindfulness or meditation. If you've ever looked at a dreamcatcher, you are looking at a mandala. Mandalas can serve as a guide for several practices, especially in Eastern culture, including meditation. It helps guide one through the process of a state of suffering to a state of joy and happiness. Mandalas can also be a visual representation of the universe, where everyone and everything is connected at one point in the center.

Every year, my family takes a trip or two on our boat to one of my favorite places on Earth, Block Island. One place on the island that we like to visit is Coast Guard Beach. We go by dinghy, pull up on the beach, and watch the boats coming into the harbor. Swimming is fun there because the beach takes a deep plunge right off the edge into dark and refreshing water. We enjoy walking the beach all the way out to the point, hoping to find a hidden glass orb (a tradition on the island) or some seals swimming offshore.

But I particularly enjoy the colorful rocks that can be found at this beach. As I walk, I can easily find rocks in all the colors and spectrums of the rainbow. In fact, a few years ago, my daughter and I spent some time creating a rock mandala on the beach with all the rainbow-colored stones. That is one of my favorite pieces of artwork I have ever created, and I'm grateful I took a picture of it to keep forever.

Last week, my family visited Block Island. We walked the beach, and I collected a rock from each color in the rainbow and put them in my pocket. It was windy and chilly, and my family didn't want to stay long enough to recreate the rainbow mandala that we had made in the past. So I happily found seven perfectly formed pebbles from all the hues in the rainbow and put them in my pocket. I even took a picture of my beautiful rocks sitting in the sand to help savor the gorgeous place in which I found these amazing rocks.

That is when the saying **"There is only one thing and we are all it"** popped into my head. I was looking at the pebbles resting in the sand, and the thought occurred to me. I am forever connected to this beach. I am these rocks, and they are me. I know that sounds a little nutty, but think about it....

If there was no island, there would be no purpose for me to be sitting on that beach.

If I had no family, there would be no one to share this natural beauty with me.

If there was no beach, there would be no place for me to come back to year after year.

If there were no trees or plants to produce oxygen, what good would my lungs be?

Connections run right through everything I can think of! Who I am today is connected with my past. And what I'll be like tomorrow depends on my present!

In many ways, I have forgotten that I am simply a very small piece of this planet we live on. I am realizing that there is no feeling of completion if there is no connection to one another, nature, ideas, feelings, and so much more.

Human connection is so powerful! Having this energy exchange between people can be powerful enough to deepen the moment, inspire change, and build trust. Research and science tell us that social associations decrease anxiety and depression, help regulate emotion, and lead to higher self-esteem.

William James, philosopher and psychologist, reminds us that, just like Block Island,

> "We are like islands in the sea, separate on the surface but connected in the deep."

So what does that mean for me? What does that mean for our world and us as a species?

We need to stop living apart and separating ourselves from others just because our opinions and lifestyles differ...just because we speak a different language, study differing religions, and have different political views. Whether we like it or not, we are all connected, just like islands in the sea or the symbolism of the mandala.

Every day, we run in our own hamster wheels, doing our own thing for our own benefit and losing sight of the fact that we are just one small part of a larger being. We need each other. Alone, we are nothing.

So, what does this realization mean for me now? I am making it a goal to make a connection every day, whether that is with nature, by taking a walk outside, enjoying the leaves falling from the trees, and the waves lapping on the shore. Or whether that is reaching out to a friend I haven't seen in a while and making time to chat or spend time together.

I need connection. **We need connection** in order to remember that we are one small part of a larger being. And without each other, without a connection to nature and this Earth, we will not survive.

I invite you to think about the last time you really stopped and took a step off your hamster wheel to enjoy the beauty of nature. If you haven't done it in a while, perhaps you can carve some time out in your day to do that now. But you really and truly need to slow your pace and find some quiet in order to do this task. What is the connection that you need in order to feel complete, and how can you seek it?

As the mandala teaches us, we are all connected at one central point, brought out as a guide to help us go from a place of suffering to one of joy and happiness. How great would the world be if we could all learn and live from this ancient symbol of the universe?

CHAPTER 12

friends are nature's way of taking care of us

I WOULD SAY THAT I AM FAIRLY OUTGOING AND CAN make friends easily. I have made friends pretty much everywhere I've been—growing up, college, every job I've held, where I live—and I am grateful for each and every connection I've ever made! I enjoy all the moments I've spent with these humans. I particularly enjoy it when I haven't spoken to a friend in a while, but we still manage to pick up right where we left off when we get back together again. These relationships bring me a lot of joy, excitement, and support. In their own individual ways, these friends have changed me for the better.

There is one particular friend that comes to mind when I think of this famous quote, commonly attributed to William Shakespeare:

"A friend is one that knows you as you are, understands where you have been, accepts what you have become, and still, gently allows you to grow."

Jen is a friend from college. We met while participating on the University of Rhode Island Sailing Team, but the best times went from there. Recently, we met for back-to-school shopping with our daughters, and over lunch, we tried to count how many years we've stayed connected. I was just turning eighteen when we met, and now we are forty-six. So, in the twenty-eight years that we have been friends, there are numerous stories about the two of us that I could tell. There's the time we created homemade peanut butter cups in Jen's dorm coffee maker for a sailing team fundraiser. Or the adventure we took to try some local flavor at a Jamaican restaurant in the middle of nowhere on our spring break. Trying out our fake IDs, taking vacations, break-ups, and parties—some stories are definitely not appropriate to tell here in this book. But I can tell you that no matter the moment, each story of us tells about a coming of age, from our college dorms and first jobs to our relationships, marriages, families, and all the highs and lows that life can bring.

One story I have about Jen and I relates to how I got to where I am, sitting right here right now, typing this story. It is a recent occurance...I think it was early spring of 2022. We decided to meet for brunch and a little shopping at Patriot's Place in Foxboro, which is the perfect meeting spot halfway between us.

I was in a pretty low place. Jen could tell by taking one look at me that I was struggling. We had been talking about it, and she knew that I wanted to leave my job as a public school classroom teacher. I was grieving the loss of this identity that I thought I had but was starting to let go of. I felt torn. My heart was with my students, my colleagues, and a profession I thought I'd have for life. But my body and my brain were thinking and feeling differently. I was stressed and overwhelmed. I was burned out, and I was questioning if staying in this job was an option moving forward.

In our conversation, I expressed that although I was considering a change in career, I had absolutely no idea how I was going to make it work. I had created this idea in my head of becoming a Social-Emotional Learning Coach. I had a passion for health and well-being from the start of my career. The first "integrated unit" that I ever created during my student teaching was on the subject of nutrition. Later, I taught health to kids in grades K-8. But those are stories for another time...

Jen knew that over the years, I had training under my belt from Responsive Classroom and RULER. Recently, I earned a certification through an organization called "Breathe for Change" to teach yoga and facilitate wellness workshops for students and teachers. I felt ready to step into this role and was lamenting that there was no such position in my district. Honestly, no position that I knew of really existed anywhere near us!

As Jen listened and asked questions over brunch, I explained the role I felt an SEL coach fulfilled. I described this dream of mine to be proactive in helping kids with mental health and well-being. As a teacher, I knew I could give kids, educators, and families tools for managing big emotions through reading books, making crafts, and discussions. I shared that I wanted to start by tutoring students but then eventually move into working in schools, helping not just kids but their teachers and families as well! My idea was that this could take some pressure off of the social workers and psychologists if these SEL skills were being taught proactively.

But making this change was a big leap. A lot of self-doubt poured out of me throughout our conversation. I don't remember exactly what was said, but I am sure I made statements such as:

- How could I just quit a job I've been doing for over twenty years?
- I don't know how to run a business.
- How can I take this pay cut?
- There aren't any jobs out there like this!
- I haven't updated my resume in years, let alone applied for a job!

- I'm old!
- Who would want me?

To me, this idea of mine seemed like a crazy leap of faith. But Jen didn't see it that way. She got really excited when I shared this idea with her. She told me she would hire me in a heartbeat for her two daughters. And she knew several of her friends that could use someone like me, as well! She asked me questions as I continued to describe my perfect job, and she began to help me form even more of an idea of what I wanted for this change in my career. But the self-doubt set in so hard that it started to solidify in my being. I wouldn't let myself be hopeful like Jen was getting for me.

Jen got even more excited when I told her that I was actively looking for a job similar to what I described. I was proud that I began to put myself out there on LinkedIn and dive head first into a job search. But my search was coming up short! This dream role of mine was really hard to find. And some of the jobs that piqued my interest didn't necessarily describe my skill set! I felt intimidated to even try to apply. Jen was firm but gentle and loving but kind with me, as she pointed out that I don't necessarily need to be a match for every skill listed on the job postings I found. She encouraged me to just go for it! She told me not to settle and suggested that I create the role for myself! Why not?

I just couldn't take what she was saying to me. She made it sound so easy! The more she told me I could, the more I said, "I can't." I started to get flustered and teary. I heard what she was saying, but I just couldn't see what she was seeing. Jen saw my vulnerability and the rawness I felt and eventually let up on the conversation, steering the subject in a different direction. We ended up having a great afternoon, but I cried my whole way home. I felt my grief combined with excitement at the possibilities Jen saw in me. But I felt hopeless. There was no way I could do what she was suggesting.

Jen sensed that I was upset and texted me later to apologize for pushing me. She felt bad that she opened up something inside of me that needed to be ripped at the seams, but I just didn't know it yet. I told her it was no big deal, but I didn't realize how big of a deal it was until much later! Jen had me thinking. It took me a bit of time, but I listened to her words of encouragement. She was right. I was ready for a change. I needed a change. And I could do it!

About four months after our brunch together, I was testing the waters of SEL tutoring, hosting a few clients throughout the summer. Seven months later, I had a business plan and put in the paperwork to create Calm Education, LLC. Eighteen months later, as I sit here and type, I have clients, I create the SEL curriculum, I record meditations, I promote myself on social media, I write a blog, and I'm working hard to get myself back into schools where I know I belong! I realize now that I didn't lose my "educator" identity....I still have my purpose, but I am just using it in a different way. This is something Jen saw in me all along. I just needed time to catch up after the gentle nudging that she gave me.

There is research that says that throughout our lives, the number and strength of our relationships have an effect on our mental and physical well-being. Social connections have many benefits, such as lower rates of anxiety and depression, higher self-esteem, greater empathy, stronger immune systems, and more trusting and cooperative relationships. In other words, surrounding ourselves with positive people can help us recover from diseases quicker and even lengthen our lives! Friends are Nature's way of taking care of us, and we need them.

As I sit here, writing this story in between answering client emails, planning lessons, and getting ready to teach a session, I can't help but feel gratitude in my heart for Jen's belief in me. While I wish I could see her more often, I know that together, we make each other stronger. That is why William Shakespeare's words resonate with me. Jen and I know each other, understand where we've been, accept each other, and gently allow each other to grow. And I am forever grateful to have her in my life.

I tell you this story to give you an opportunity to reflect on your relationships. Do you embrace the people in your life that inspire, empower, and motivate you to be your best? When you finish reading this story, I invite you to take time to simply nurture the healthy relationships you have in your life with the people who make you feel good. Life gets busy, but making space for you and your friends to spend time together is the best (and easiest) form of self-care. Call them, text them, make time for them, and tell your friends how grateful you are for their presence in your life. And...be well.

CHAPTER 13

---

far (but not so distant) friends

HAVE YOU EVER TRULY THOUGHT ABOUT WHAT FRIEND-ship means to you? What do you look for in a friend? What makes someone worth keeping in your inner circle?

Loyalty
Love
Understanding
Acceptance
Patience
.....more?

Friendship, like every relationship, is a two-way street. Friends care about each other, support one another, and accept each other's differences. Friends enjoy spending time together and bring out the very best in each other. We miss friends when they are gone. And we get excited to see them when they return.

There are very few people in my life that I can remember meeting for the first time. My friend Suzi is one of them. About three years ago, we moved to New Zealand. My husband was working there, my kids got to attend school, and I took a year off from my teaching position, so I got to be solely a mom, exploring a foreign country with my family. We moved during the COVID years, so we spent two weeks in managed isolation before we could acclimate into the Kiwi world.

We had just gotten out of isolation and were seeing our neighborhood and home for the first time, and we met our real estate agent at the house we decided to rent for the year. We were just getting a tour and unpacking our things when I heard a voice coming from the front door. I went to see who it was and saw a woman standing there with her cute little black dog. Little did I know that this woman would become a close friend…our families would enjoy time together, and I would fall in love with her dog, Charlie.

This woman introduced herself as "Suzi," and I immediately recognized her American accent with a tiny Kiwi twang. She explained that she was from Pennsylvania but was living with her husband and children (all Kiwi) in New Zealand. I knew right away that we were going to hit it off.

The entire year that I lived in New Zealand, Suzi lived next door to me. We talked every day, walked and attended a yoga class regularly, and supported each other through occasional COVID lockdowns. My favorite memories were with her out in front of our houses with a glass of wine, sitting socially distanced in our lawn chairs and chatting until the sun went down.

Suzi introduced me to her friends. She made cupcakes with my daughter on her birthday. She had her kids babysit mine so that my husband and I could go out together. She came to our Halloween party dressed as a cupcake. She hosted a gingerbread house-making workshop for my kids and their friends over the holidays. She gave me advice and recommendations for things to do while we were living there and became my closest friend in New Zealand.

I knew when I left that Suzi was going to be the person that I would miss the most. She drove us to the airport the day we moved home. And I teared up at having to say goodbye to her. I had no idea when I would see her again, but we promised each other that we would stay in touch and visit each other when we could.

Staying in touch with someone on the other side of the world and a day ahead of you is next to impossible. But Suzi and I make it happen like champs! It is amazing that she is able to be so close to me even though she is thousands of miles from my presence. Thank goodness for WhatsApp! We can text each other, call, and FaceTime regularly. And I look forward to each and every conversation that usually turns into over an hour of gabbing and catching up every time!

This Christmas, Suzi's husband reached out to me and asked if I would be around to visit with her this summer. He planned to get her a gift to come home to the USA, tour New York City, visit her family, and have some fun with me. This felt like a Christmas present for me, as well! I couldn't wait and immediately began planning our short time together.

When she arrived this week, I was busting out of my skin with excitement. I couldn't wait to give her a hug and welcome her into my home. I couldn't wait to see how much her kids had grown and for her to see the same in my children. And what a week it was! We jammed a lot into the four days we spent together—a trip to Boston, a tour in Newport, and a few trips out on the boat for a motor and a sail! It was incredible! And it didn't feel like I hadn't seen her in three years. We picked up right where we left off...pure joy and fun! Just like friends should be!

Sometimes, it feels like Suzi and I have been friends since childhood. It is crazy how sometimes you just 'click' with others....like we were meant to find each other and make a connection. I can't express how grateful I am for her friendship.... It is a rare friendship that can sustain such a distance, with only monthly communication, and pick up right where it left off.

Having Suzi and her kids visit this week was a gift. There was no awkwardness, no gaps in conversation to fill...we carried on together like we were never apart. And to me, that is a true friend.

I don't know when we will see each other again, but I know one thing for certain...there **will be** a next time. I am secretly hoping our reunion will be in New Zealand again.... I love that place, and I certainly left a piece of my heart there when I came back to the States. But I know Suzi is holding on to it and guarding it well. I can't wait to see what the future has in store for our friendship...it is going to be a good one! As someone wise said,

> "It is friends we meet along the way that help us appreciate the journey."

And that is certainly true with my friendship with Suzi. And I am forever grateful.

CHAPTER 14

dirty chocolate

WHEN I WAS TEACHING IN A PUBLIC SCHOOL CLASSroom, I spent quite a bit of time at the start of a school year getting to know my students and letting them learn about me. We played games, shared stories, and had fun together as a way of breaking the ice and building our community.

One of my favorite games was to give the students a quiz about me. It would ask them questions about things such as my family, my interests, and my hobbies.

One particular question focused on my love of chocolate and my favorite brand, Lindor! This question often led to many students bringing me Lindt Chocolate treats on special occasions, which I really relished in.

One year, one of my students took this quiz and went home to ask her parents if she could bring me some of my favorite chocolate. The only problem was that she couldn't remember the name of my favorite brand. She expressed this to her mom, who tried to help by doing some research. They searched through different brands of chocolate, but none of them rang a bell.

The only thing she could remember was that the name sounded like it was dirty...get it? Lindt...lint...dirt.

So, what did the family decide to do? They Googled "Dirty Chocolate." And boy, were they in for a surprise! The things that popped up on the screen were eye-opening for my fourth-grade student. Take a moment to think about what could possibly come up if you type "dirty" and "chocolate" into a search engine. Yup! It was nowhere near appropriate for a fourth-grader!!

The next day, my student's mom came into my classroom to ask me directly exactly what I told my students the day before. What was the name of my favorite chocolate?

She told me the story of their Google experience and everything that popped up on their screen...some of which she had to shield from her child's eyes!

When I explained to my student's mom that my favorite chocolate was *Lindt*, it took us a second to understand the connection to *dirty*. When it finally clicked in our brains, we were both in stitches, laughing to the point of tears! I couldn't believe that my conversation about Lindor Chocolates came to this!

After we explained my favorite brand of chocolate to my fourth grader, she thought it was funny, as well. She had us all rolling when she said, "YES! Lindt! Like belly button lint!"

I knew immediately that this was a story I would never forget.

Needless to say, the next day, I had a GIANT bag of Lindor Chocolates on my desk. But the best part was the picture that my student drew to go along with it. It was a drawing of me holding a piece of chocolate in one hand and my finger on my belly button with the other hand! I laughed out loud. This child had an incredible sense of humor!

Moments like these remind me of the importance of building connections and relationships with others. That one small question on a silly quiz gave a reason for this child's parents to reach out to me.

The joke of "Lint" chocolate brought a side to my student's sense of humor that I may not have otherwise seen.

The pressure on public school teachers to get their students to perform is real. They are given a schedule of lessons and assessments that their district (and sometimes the state) must adhere to. Often, teachers start getting into challenging academic content with their students within the first few days of school.

And then we all wonder why we start to see inappropriate behaviors from our students almost immediately...

When I took my Responsive Classroom teacher courses, I learned about the importance of the first six weeks of school. These few weeks are a time of introductions for our students—we introduce students to each other, to the school community, and to the expectations we hold for them. We introduce them to routines that will help them take care of their environment and each other! During this time, it is important to create a safe climate for our students so they feel a sense of belonging.

The way I see it, this time is the most important few weeks of the school year!

But school schedules and academic expectations aren't always created with this in mind, leaving students feeling like they can't connect and they can't follow or even remember the routines, which leads to frustration and overwhelm.

And then the behavior problems kick in.

No human can learn in a place where they feel they don't belong. If we feel stressed, frustrated, and overwhelmed every day, it is going to impact learning. Not only does building community and making connections in a classroom setting prevent behavior issues, but it can also help increase rates of academic success! There is a lot of research to support this, as well.

So, how does a classroom teacher use the first six weeks of school to build community while trying to adhere to their school district's academic expectations?

The best they can.

It is important for teachers to remember that they are professionals. They know the needs of their students more than anyone in the school setting. They deserve the freedom to make professional decisions on what is best for their classroom and student learning.

Teachers need to give themselves permission to do exactly that... whatever it takes to make students feel comfortable, accepted, and ready to learn. And if that means adjusting the calendar to meet the needs of the students in their classroom, then that is what they should professionally be allowed to do.

As a classroom teacher, I tried to remind myself that what happens within the four walls of my classroom *is all on me*. It is important to remember that as a classroom teacher, it is my duty to do my best for my students, and I can do that in the best way I see fit.

I also liked to remind myself that no one can learn if they aren't comfortable. Districts want to see student scores increase, and there is no better way to do it than by building relationships and creating a thriving classroom community.

So, if that means that you create inside jokes about dirty chocolate with your students and their parents, so be it! Be sure to take as many opportunities as possible to laugh...that shared laughter with the kiddos is what will get you all through!

You'll feel positive about what you are teaching.

Your students will learn.

Together, you will create a sense of belonging for everyone.

To me, that describes the perfect school, the best teacher, and the most ideal classroom...who wouldn't want that?

CHAPTER 15

you couldn't pay me

YOU COULDN'T PAY ME TO GO BACK TO MY MIDDLE school years. I tell my daughter this all the time, and I don't think I am the only adult who feels this way. Middle School is rough...like *Lord of the Flies* rough. At times, it can feel like a bunch of kids stranded on an island, making up their own societal rules and resulting in disaster.

My daughter is in the thick of middle school. She enters seventh grade in just a few weeks, and we are playing the summer waiting game right now to see who her teachers will be and if her friends will be with her. She often expresses that while she has friends, she doesn't feel like she fits into any particular group of girls.

I remember this feeling.

I never had one particular group of friends. Through middle school and high school, I floated around many different groups. I hung out with the kids who played instruments in the marching band. I hung out with kids who played sports. I participated in the theater program and hung out with those kids, too. My friends were on the student council and in the recycling club. I even had friends outside of school from my summer sailing team that I enjoyed so much. And, of course, I had a few friends who had been with me since elementary school.

I remember seeing kids that were *always* together. They went to football games and sat in the same section. They went to dances together and hung out on the dance floor in one solid group. They played on sports teams and hung out in after-school clubs together. They were "it" by everyone's standards....they dressed the right way, looked the right way, and were the envy of everyone. While I floated between all these groups, I never actually fit in their circle.

It wasn't that kids didn't like me. I think a lot of kids enjoyed my company. I always had someone to go out to the movies with or to come hang out at my house. I had boyfriends and went to pretty much every school function.

But I wasn't one of the popular kids.

And honestly, while that was OK with me at the time, I know that deep down inside of me, somewhere, I always wished I was one of them.

I think that is the *ultimate rock ballad* of most kids, especially in middle school.

...to be popular.

Because if you are popular, you are accepted by everyone.

Kids notice you.

They envy you.

And there is power in that.

I really wish I could go back to my middle school self and rethink this kind of power-sucking way of life. I wish I could ask my younger self, "What does it *really* mean to be popular?"

If my middle school self couldn't answer that question, I'd try to help her define popularity. The first thing I'd tell her is that to be popular is a lot of pressure. The popular group has one group of friends, and they are put up on a pedestal by everyone. And while that feels great at the moment, middle school kids can very easily take that away from anyone.

I'd say to my younger self, "It doesn't take much for middle schoolers to decide you're not 'it' anymore. One small disagreement with a friend within that clique, and you're out. And what are you left with?"

I'd tell her that the best part about having several different groups of friends is that there is always someone there to hang out with. I'd say, "If a disagreement erupts or there is drama within one of your groups of friends, it is always possible to float to another group for a bit until the argument blows over. And if one group decides you aren't 'in' anymore, there are other groups to fall back on. In other words, having different friends in different places means there is always someone there for you."

I'm not sure the same can be said about the popular kids. It may feel that way at times, but it isn't always the case.

Popularity also means that there are a whole lot of unwritten rules that one must follow. Popular kids have to act a certain way and dress a certain way...if they don't, they're not "in." That can feel like a lot of pressure!

I'd tell myself that having several different groups of friends means you can be who you want to be, when you want to be them. There is no one telling you what to do, how to dress, or how to behave. I'd tell myself, "You can be unequivocally you! And there is a lot of freedom in that. Middle school is all about figuring out who you are, what you believe in, and who you want to surround yourself with. It is nice to be able to choose that for yourself."

I didn't see any of this when I was in middle school. No one does. I really wish I had someone to show me. But let's face it...I probably wouldn't have listened anyway.

I know perfectly well that this means that I have a very important job with my middle school-aged daughter. Since I can very strongly understand how she feels, I need to first acknowledge her emotions as they come up. They are valid, and I need to help her see that I know and understand them.

But most importantly, I need to keep encouraging her to "do her thing" and "show the world who she is" without the influence of others. When I was a kid, the popular girls wore Benneton and Esprit. Today, it's Lululemon. While a lot has changed for kids throughout the years, the need to fit in with what you wear and how you look hasn't changed all that much. I need to remind my daughter how beautiful she is...inside and out...Lululemon or not!

Through this conversation, I need to let my daughter know what true friendship means. I need to show her that true friends accept you for who you are, what you look like, what you enjoy, and what you wear. I need to model my friendships for her and see that adult humans don't depend on the superficial stuff as much as they did when they were in middle school...at least, we hope. And if I find someone superficial in my circle, I keep my cautious, yet polite, distance...just as she can in middle school.

I need to remind my daughter how friends should make us feel. Friends should lift us up, make us feel good about ourselves, and feel accepted. If that's not happening, it is time to let those 'friends' keep walking. It is OK to be kind, but we don't need to waste our energy in those circles.

But at the same time, I need to remind my daughter that she and her friends are all in this crazy middle school time together...everyone is feeling self-conscious, misunderstood, and hormonal. And everyone will make mistakes. When a friend is disrespectful, it is OK to hear them out rather than write them off.....accept apologies and keep moving forward. No one is perfect, including her.

As parents, if we can get through the middle school years with our children, we can get through anything! When our kids hit this time in their lives, it puts us right back in it, even if we wouldn't take a million dollars to be there. Be patient, be understanding, and do your best.

Your kids will get through it, and so will you! It's all about patience, love, and grace...keep going!

PART 4

lessons in family

CHAPTER 16

in the spirit of thanksgiving...

THERE WAS A BRIEF PERIOD OF TIME WHEN MY FAMILY packed up a few things, put them on a container ship, boarded a plane, and went to live in New Zealand. This was probably one of the best experiences we've ever had as a family. We lived there through COVID, where the country was pretty much living freely, and the rest of the world lived behind masks and plexiglass shields. My kids freely went to school, we rented a house, and my husband worked as a designer and engineer for a sailing team.

While we were there, I absolutely fell in love with the country of New Zealand. I honestly can't say enough good things about it. One thing that struck me from the moment I stepped on their soil was the different terms in the language that they use. I particularly enjoyed the term "partner."

Back at home, not many people referred to their significant other as their partner. To me, that term was confusing...I couldn't tell if the couple was married, gay, or simply dating. But it seemed that everyone around me in New Zealand referred to their better half as their "partner." At first, this was uncomfortable for me. I didn't connect with this term. I had never really used it!

But now that I am back in the USA, I have to be honest...I miss being referred to as Andrew's partner. And I miss calling him *my partner*. Why? Because I have really learned to appreciate the meaning behind this term.

There is a famous quote by author and relationship coach Barbara DeAngelis that says,

> "Marriage is not a noun; it's a verb. It isn't something you get. It's something you do."

Let me explain...fast forward a few years from our New Zealand experience, and I find myself in an entirely new place. I have since left my job of over twenty years and started my own business. We came home from New Zealand, and I worked for one more year as a public school classroom teacher. Throughout that year, I floated the idea to Andrew of leaving my position...just up and quitting! That meant a HUGE pay cut. But Andrew could tell I was ready for a change. He was incredibly supportive. He helped me rewrite my resume, market myself on LinkedIn, and brainstorm ideas for my business. At the end of the school year, he agreed to take a huge pay cut from our family and allow me to go on this crazy adventure.

After I made this change, I continued to get support from Andrew. He helped me rearrange our upstairs exercise room into a mini classroom and office. He began to take on more bill-paying responsibilities since he was the primary money-maker in the family. He continued to listen to and support my ideas for my new business. And he reads and talks to me about my silly blogs, so I know he reads them!

The level of support and guidance I have gotten from Andrew in the last year or so is amazing. But that is not all that Andrew is to me...he is truly my partner. Together, we have remodeled a house with our own two pairs of hands, changed diapers, and stayed up at all hours of the night to feed and take care of our babies. Now that our kids are getting older and more independent, he still shares the responsibilities. When I cook dinner, he cleans and puts away dishes. We say goodnight to our kids together. We split the driving between activities. We both created and continue to craft this family in true partner fashion.

I think that a partnership is the perfect way to describe my relationship with Andrew. We are a team, and we are in this together, which is why, as I look back on it, I can't imagine calling Andrew anything else. The word "husband" doesn't quite have the same meaning behind it as "partner." There is so much more substance behind Andrew and me than husband and wife.

I work hard to maintain a daily gratitude practice where I share all that I am thankful for. This is beneficial to my health, both physically and mentally. So, in the spirit of Thanksgiving, the art of appreciation, and the hope that I inspire my readers, I am writing all of this today to express my gratitude for my partner, Andrew.

I would not be sitting here right now, typing this story and creating this business if it weren't for him.

I wouldn't be the mom that I am to our two gorgeous kids if it weren't for him.

I wouldn't have this awesome place to live if it weren't for him.

We wouldn't go on our favorite sailing vacations if it weren't for him.

I wouldn't have the love and joy I have in my life if it weren't for him.

I wouldn't cook an awesome Thanksgiving meal without him.

I wouldn't have someone that makes me laugh like he does.

...and I wouldn't trade in my partner for anything in the world! I can't wait to see what the future has in store for us because together, it feels like we can do anything. I want to thank my New Zealand experience for giving me the language to express what we are together. Andrew truly is my greatest partner...the one that knows me best, my biggest cheerleader, the one that makes me smile the biggest, my greatest source of comfort, and my favorite.... And for that, I am grateful!

CHAPTER 17

the universe and the message she sends

I HAVE A SISTER WHO IS VERY SPECIFIC ABOUT WHAT I call her. She doesn't like to be called my "older sister." She also doesn't like the term "big sister." So, instead, I chose to call her my "best sister," and she seemed ok with that. It doesn't matter that my **best sister** also happens to be my *only sister*. Kim is truly the best sister I could have ever asked for.

When my best sister turned fifty, my mom and I thought it would be fun to take a trip, just the three of us. We have done plenty of outings and overnights together, but we haven't really gone away for an extended time with just us.

My mom and I decided to plan a fun trip to Bermuda last May. We made arrangements to stay in Boston the night before so we could catch an early flight without having to wake up in what could feel like the middle of the night. And we got reservations at the Hamilton Princess—a gorgeous Bermuda resort with access to beaches and the town. We couldn't wait!

But then, when the time for the trip arrived, my mom came down with an awful case of Pneumonia. There was no way we could make this trip happen together. My mom wanted Kim and I to go without her, but that wasn't even a negotiation. We couldn't enjoy this vacation without our mom, so we decided to cancel our plans and postpone our trip.

Shortly after, when my mom recovered, we made new arrangements. We re-booked our trip exactly the way it was originally planned, but this time, we decided to go the last weekend of October. We knew the weather would be a little cooler than in May, but we decided that was ok…it was still better than New England, especially with all the rain we've had each weekend!

We spent the summer thinking about what we were going to bring with us and what we could do in Bermuda other than going to the beach. When my birthday came, my mom gave me a cute little travel bag for my toiletries that I could use for the trip. Nothing was going to stop us this time. I mean, what were the odds, right?!

For about two weeks before we left, I obsessively watched the weather in Hamilton, Bermuda. It was going to be perfect—in the high seventies with lots of sunshine! But then the time came for us to start packing, so I needed to be sure I had the right clothes for the weather. When I clicked on my weather app, I saw a prediction that we knew was always a possibility, but the odds were low due to it being the end of the season. A hurricane was barrelling toward Bermuda! It looked like it would go to the East, and I started to feel hopeful. It'll be fine…maybe just a little wind and rain on our first day, but then things will clear up.

As we continued to watch the weather, we began to realize that things were *not* going to clear up. The hurricane was downgraded to a tropical storm, but it looked like it was going to be a direct hit. We soon realized that we would be flying into the island with gusty winds over fifty mph. And there would be rain the whole weekend. It was possible that the only sun we would see would be on the day before we were due to turn around and come home. Was it worth spending all this money for this kind of weather? And would the plane even fly in all that wind? The thought of our airplane landing in a storm gave me knots in my stomach.

We began to feel nervous and realized that a decision needed to be made about whether or not we would go on the trip. But the decision was easily made for us when my dad came down with a cold. He was feverish and tired, so he decided to take a test. We couldn't believe it when my dad tested positive for COVID. That was all we needed to hear! It was imperative to cancel our trip. With a tropical storm and the likelihood that my mom would have COVID symptoms within the next few days, we decided not to go *once again*.

Jokingly, my mom, my sister, and I all agreed that the universe was sending us a message. Maybe Bermuda wasn't where we were supposed to celebrate together. The universe tried to tell us this back in May, but we didn't listen when we re-booked. So she had to be loud and clear by sending us a storm and sickness to keep us back.

The question is, why? Why doesn't the universe want us to go to Bermuda? I thought about that the whole weekend I was home instead of enjoying a beach vacation with the two women who know me best. I thought...

Maybe the universe is telling us that we can celebrate by being together but keep things a little more simple.

Maybe we don't need to obsess over what we will pack or what the weather will be like.

Maybe we don't need to spend a lot of money.

Maybe we don't need to exhaust ourselves with airline travel.

Maybe we can plan something a little more simple and still enjoy time away together.

Thinking about the universe's message made me feel like my brain was going to places a little "out there." But then I remembered what scientist, mathematician, physicist, and astronomer Sir Isaac Newton said,

"Nature is pleased with simplicity."

Isaac Newton studied nature with a realistic eye and noticed patterns, beauty, art, predictability, and simplicity in everything that is in our natural world. There is nothing we can do to stop nature's tropical storms or germs affecting our bodies. They are going to simply occur, whether we like it or not.

But we can listen to nature's universal messages. I truly believe that nature is constantly talking to us. All we have to do is recognize, listen, and decode what she's saying. How often do we hear those little voices and see the signs but choose to forge ahead anyway? All those "maybes" I was thinking about are truths about my sister's birthday trip. Maybe...

We can celebrate together and keep things simple.

We don't need to obsess over what to pack.

The weather will be what it will be, and we can't predict that.

We don't need to spend a lot of money.

We don't need to exhaust ourselves in our travels.

We can plan something simple and still enjoy our time together.

We are so lucky that the universe and nature have given us this gift of time together. It honestly doesn't matter what we do as long as we are with each other. Time is fragile, so it is important to take advantage of it.

Ironically, the day we were supposed to leave for our trip, my mom did eventually come down with COVID. The rest of us haven't had any symptoms yet, but only time (and nature) will tell! Anyway, Kim and I did spend time together over the weekend picking apples, doing a little shopping, and having lunch together in Newport. We still enjoyed part of the weekend in each other's company without the stress of the weather, sickness, or overall travel. It was nice to be with each other, enjoying the warmth and the sunshine of Fall back home in Rhode Island.

I was supposed to be flying home from Bermuda today, but instead, I am writing this story, sipping some warm tea, and listening to the chilly New England rain fall on my roof. But that's OK. Because I know as soon as everyone is feeling better, we will make new plans. And we will listen to what the universe is telling us and take advantage of time together without exhaustion, expense, or worries. And, of course, I can't wait to celebrate the best sister that nature gave me!

CHAPTER 18

gotta love teen spirit

MY SON IS GOING TO BE SIXTEEN YEARS OLD VERY soon. He's my firstborn...the boy that made me a mom to begin with. I absolutely adore him, and there are times when the mommy inside of me just wants to hug him and smother him with love. But he won't have ANY of that...at all.

Any parents of teens out there that can relate? Please tell me I'm not alone.

My teen gives me very few hugs or physical affection. When he was young, and I would go out for only a few hours and come home, I used to get a run, leap, and bound into my arms for a "welcome back." Now I'm lucky if I get a grunt, a head nod, and a "Hey, Mom."

I don't know...maybe he thinks he's too old for hugs. Or maybe he thinks he's too cool. I'm pretty sure there is something biological or developmental about why teens stop hugging their moms...but man, it isn't easy!

So what does this hug-deprived mother do?? I try to look for affection from my son where I can find it.

Recently, I have truly enjoyed car rides with him. He's on a sailing team that meets about an hour away from our house. My husband usually drives one way, and I drive the other. Most of the time, I am on the afternoon pick-up end of things. When he gets in the car, he is usually full of life and energy, willing to talk openly about the highlights of his day. I let him chat away, occasionally offering opinions and always asking follow-up questions. Sometimes, I ask questions I already know the answer to, just to show him my interest. My favorite part is when he asks for my input or asks me questions about things. We usually stop for a snack that he shares with me while we chat. The car ride home goes fairly quickly. Let's face it...it isn't often that I get an hour alone with my teenage son! And he seems fairly enthusiastic about spending that time with me, as well. So, I'll take that as a verbal hug!

There is a lot of research out there that says kids (teens and adults, too) need physical affection every day. They say...

4 hugs a day for survival
8 hugs a day for maintenance
And....
12 hugs a day for growth.

That seems like an awful lot!! I'm not sure either of my kids are getting that from me...or honestly even want that! So, I've decided to interact with my kids in a way that shows hugs can come in all shapes, sizes, and forms.

Most of the time, my "hugs" with my teen are not the traditional kind. I may tousle his hair here or there. Occasionally, we'll give each other a knuckle bop or a high five. When we're joking with each other, I may give an elbow nudge his way. Or I might lean on his shoulder from the side for a second or two (I can do that now that he's taller than me!). If I'm lucky, I'll get a side hug. But I really do truly melt when he lets me give him a real, traditional hug...even if it's a short one!

- Hugs are calming.
- Hugs make us feel safe and secure.
- They can improve our mood.
- And reduce depression.
- They can build relationships and heal.

My son is growing up...two more years, and he is legally an adult. In a few short months, he will be driving around town by himself! He wants his physical space from his parents, and I get it! But no matter what he does...I do everything I can to let him know that I love him.

I always make a point to say goodnight. Either I find him in the house, or I'll text him to let him know I'm going to bed. Oftentimes, he comes to find me to say goodnight in person if I do that. And when I tell my son I love him, he always says it back. Honestly, there's nothing better than that.

I still want to hug my teenage son. And every once in a while, I'll ask for a hug, and he will give it to me. Every once in a *long* while, I will get a spontaneous hug from him, which I cherish more than most things...

So, what do I say to all my fellow moms of teens out there? Keep finding ways to let your kids know you love them...sometimes the little ways add up BIG! And honestly, I won't blame you if you sneak in a little hug or snuggle before you wake them up in the morning. After all, moms need love, too!

Am I right?!

CHAPTER 19

take credit for the good things, too!

WHEN MY KIDS WERE LITTLE, THEY HAD MOMENTS where they were naughty. It is hard to imagine now because they have grown up and matured so much since then. As tweens and teens, my kids have become very thoughtful and kind. They have good manners. They know how to sit respectfully at a dinner table in a restaurant. They work hard in school. And they are good to their family and friends.

But when they were young, they were self-centered, often thinking about what they needed and wanted. Developmentally, that is what they were supposed to do! But that made it tricky to visit family and friends or go out to dinner. It was inevitable that, at some point, one of them would do something rude or have a meltdown. And I would be left in a pile of my own sweat (and sometimes tears) about it all!

The worst was if I got a call from someone at school reporting to me that one of my kids did something wrong…maybe they snatched something out of someone else's hands during play centers in preschool, resulting in a minor scuffle. Or, they had trouble sitting still on the carpet in Kindergarten and had to walk the halls with the principal to get a little movement break. Perhaps they broke something or fought the entire time that they visited with their grandparents. Those calls were THE WORST! And they often left me thinking...

> What did I do wrong?
> Everyone must think I am a bad parent!
> I need to do something different to get these kids to behave better!

I would beat myself up over how their behavior was a reflection of my parenting...that if I changed my parenting style, they would be better kids. I worried what people in a restaurant thought of me as a parent. I apologized to teachers and staff on behalf of my kids' behavior. It was pure agony, the pressure and blame I put on myself when my kids made mistakes.

I credited myself for the bad behavior of my children so many times. But you know what? I *never* gave myself credit for the things they did right!

Sometimes, we would go out to a nice family dinner at a restaurant, and everything would be peaceful. Or, my kids would spend the weekend with their grandparents and have a lovely time together. Even better, the school would call to tell me how great my child behaved that day or to share their awesome hard work. And NOT ONCE would I ever think....

> What did I do right?
> Everyone must think I am the BEST parent!
> I need to keep doing what I'm doing as a parent because it rocks!

I never allowed myself to feel positive about how all the good things they did were a reflection of my parenting. I never thought that anyone was looking at me thinking, "Wow! How does she do it?" I never once gave myself credit for all the hard work it took to be there for my kids.

I am writing all of this in hopes that you can relate. And you understand the shame and embarrassment I felt when my kids did something wrong. And maybe you realize that, like me, you passed the credit to someone or something else when your kids were amazing.

If this is you, I am going to tell you something I wish someone had told me...*take credit for the good things, too!*

Kids will always reach a new milestone...maybe you will watch them graduate or win an award at school. Or maybe you will watch them in a performance of some kind. Perhaps you will get to see some really awesome school work of theirs in the classroom and on the sports field. Whatever it is, acknowledge that these things make you feel proud! And that pride comes from you...YOUR PARENTING SKILLS!!

Don't forget to take a moment to not only be grateful for your kids and all the good things they do but also to show love and kindness to yourself. While they are their own people, your kids have been molded in some way by you. Literally, your blood, sweat, and tears have been behind every single thing your child has accomplished. Please don't forget to take a moment to give yourself credit where credit is due.

Because you're absolutely and incredibly amazing!

And so are your kids....

After all, they are going to be your greatest achievement.

Now that is totally worth cheering for!!

CHAPTER 20

better to have loved and lost...

THIS SUMMER, MY SON SAILED IN A REGATTA OUT ON Cape Cod, and we decided to make a family weekend out of it. While we were there, my daughter and I decided to take a little afternoon trip out to Nantucket on the high-speed ferry.

I feel like if you own a dog and plan to visit Nantucket, it is a rule that you *must* take your dog with you. We don't own a dog, but I know my daughter wishes we did.

This is a far cry from how things used to be...when she was a baby, she was horribly afraid of any dog that came near her. Not just a little fearful...a full-on, red-faced, sweaty lip, shaking kind of scared! My husband and I had dogs when we first met and always planned to have more as part of our family in the future. But we knew perfectly well that if we brought a dog into the house, we would give my daughter a life of panic attacks.

So we decided to get her a cat instead.

I never had cats as a kid, so I didn't know what I was in for. I figured they were aloof and independent and weren't as attached as dogs can be. *Boy, was I wrong!* We picked a cat that is like a dog in kitty clothing. He fetches and snuggles. He sleeps at our feet and greets us at the door. He begs for treats. He was the perfect addition to our family. And the trick worked! Now, my daughter is fully in love with every type of animal, especially dogs.

So, while we were on the ferry, my daughter had a grand old time! She oogled, petted, and shook paws with every dog that looked her way through the entire one-hour ride across to the island. There were a whole bunch of dogs to choose from! Like I said, taking your dog to Nantucket is *a thing*.

When we returned to the mainland, she couldn't stop talking about how badly she wanted a dog. She began to notice every dog that was in our vicinity, daydreaming about what kind of dog she would want, what she would name it, and how well it would get along with our cat.

Like I said, I grew up with dogs. I had one in my family when I was a kid. In college, I adopted my own dog, who lived with me in my rented college house. He even drove across the country to spend a few years in California with me, as well. My husband also had a dog when we first met. In fact, I joke that I fell in love with his dog before I fell in love with him...which might not be a joke at all!

We are dog people. I never imagined a married life with kids and no dog! I can't believe we don't have a dog yet! Especially since my daughter has become so comfortable with them. When she started to ask (more like beg) for a dog this weekend, I had a whole slew of excuses....

> We wouldn't be able to travel like we do right now.
> Dogs require a lot more work and attention than cats!
> Dogs shed!
> Our cat will never get along with a dog.

When we got our cat, the deal with my kids was that we wouldn't get one unless they promised to feed it and empty its litter box.

Whelp...that didn't work out so well for us. My kids *very rarely* open up a can of cat food for the little guy. And I'm pretty sure they have *no idea* where we even keep the litter box.

So, if we have a dog in the house, I am fairly certain that I will be the one that will walk it. And we will get into a pattern where we feed it because the kids are never up early enough in the morning and are so busy during the evenings.

So I gave my daughter a whole lecture on this...and I received a lecture in return on how they will do better helping out with the dog.

I saw this cartoon the other day about dog lovers who don't actually have their own dog. It was captioned "me with other people's dogs," and it shows a woman lying on the ground, surrounded by dogs licking her face.

That's me.

I am a lot like my daughter on the ferry. When I see a dog, I can't help myself. I start to talk to it in a high-pitched voice. I get on the ground with it. I have a full-on conversation with it, imagining that it is talking back to me. I shake its paw, pet its belly, and give it a good bum rub. Dogs love me, and I am a total sucker for the wet nose and fluffy tail.

So I have been thinking about this a lot. As a self-proclaimed "dog person," why don't I want to get a dog?

Because when you get a dog, you know two things...you're going to fall in love with it, and it's going to die one day. You knowingly walk headfirst into a heartbreak. It is the basic madness of dog ownership.

My dog in college was a black lab named Guinness. He literally grew up with me. He was my buddy. He went everywhere I went. He watched me graduate from college, get my first job, get married, and get pregnant. When I was pregnant with my son, he would lie next to me with his head on my belly. When he kicked, my dog's head would bobble up and down. When I cried, he licked my tears and snuggled with me. I don't know what I would have done without him in my twenties.

When I went into the hospital to have my son, my dog was close to twelve years old, and he immediately went downhill. My husband couldn't stay with me in the hospital because he needed to go home to take care of my dog. When I came home with my new baby boy, Guinness's hip dysplasia was so bad he couldn't walk to greet me. My husband had to pick him up and take him outside. We put him on the ground near my son in his bucket car seat. Guinness scooted over to my son and rested his head in the bucket, much like he did on my belly when I was pregnant.

Seeing that he couldn't walk, I knew right then and there that I would have to put him down. He was in pain. He wasn't living a good life anymore. Literally, the day after my son was born, I had to bring him to the vet and say goodbye. He was my first kid....

....and my heart broke.

My husband and I had already put his dog down a few years before. This was equally as heartbreaking...and to do it a second time was just too unbearable.

I swore I would never do it again.

And now here I am with a daughter begging me to get her a dog. I don't *ever* want her to feel the way I felt when I put Guinness down. I don't *ever* want her to experience that kind of pain. And I don't think I can put myself through it again.

That's why I can't invite another dog into my life.

But then I think about my dog in cat's clothing...the cat that we got our daughter to warm her up to the idea of a dog in the house. And even though I know that he will most likely live a lot longer than our dogs, my heartbreak will be equal when it is his time. Just like a dog, we will outlive him. And we will all feel a little emptier when he is gone. I can't spare my kids from that heartbreak.

I know perfectly well that we are in denial about that. In all of our minds, our cat will live forever...just like I felt when I adopted Guinness. We go into these things excited about a new life in our home...we don't think about the end; why would we?

Shouldn't it be the same when it comes to the possibility of adopting a dog? Can I think about a full life with this animal rather than the pain of the end?

I'm not sure....

I don't do that with the humans in my life.

I don't wish that I never met them and got to know them so I can spare myself the heartache of losing them....

....that heartache is real.

And it hurts.

But then I remind myself that by getting a pet, I am teaching my kids to love. The world needs a whole lot more of that these days. After all, Alfred Lord Tennyson did say,

> "'Tis better to have loved and lost,
> than never to have loved at all."

This I definitely believe to be true. I wouldn't trade my time with Guinness for the world. He is at the center of many of my young adulthood memories. While they hurt, those high times were worth the pain.

So does this mean I'll get my family a dog? I don't know...if I keep writing, I may convince myself that it'll be OK. All the other excuses were true...traveling will be more difficult, we will have to divide and conquer on taking care of the dog *as a family*, and it is a must that the dog gets along with our cat.

This is a pretty tall order...so we'll have to see. However, I am happy to have my daughter with me so that we can love everyone else's dogs in the meantime. So feel free to send your pups our way for some extra love and attention anytime! We'll always dish it out for our furry friends!

PART 5

lessons in roadblocks

CHAPTER 21

the balance

I HAVE OPENED A DOCUMENT TO START WRITING THIS story about three times today. And each time, I get distracted and find something else that needs my attention. It hasn't gotten done, and now here I am, at the eleventh hour, trying to get my ideas down. Wait...ideas? What ideas? I have no idea what I want to write about today....

The problem is that I am highly distracted this week. Actually, I am going to be honest. I have been extremely distracted for a few weeks now. The balance of organizing activities, packing bags, planning rides, and making sure my family is where they need to be has been a lot for me to manage this summer. My son is on a sailing team that is over an hour's drive each way. And my daughter has a different schedule each week, depending on the activity she has going on. I have been struggling to maintain a regular routine.

I know I can't be the only mom that feels like a very underpaid Uber driver this summer. I feel like that is all I do—DRIVE! As soon as I drop one kiddo off, another one needs to be picked up, and the cycle continues. I find myself doing my work in short bursts of time... an hour here, fifteen minutes there....

It is truly amazing how much I can get done when I only have minutes to work! I am like a machine, grinding everything that I need to do out in a very short amount of time. But other days, this crazy pace that I've been keeping becomes wearing, and when I have a moment alone, I just want to veg. It is also amazing how fast time can fly when I begin to waste it by puttering around the house, browsing the internet, and checking my social media feeds.

I have come to the conclusion that I am struggling to keep a good work-life-family balance this summer. And when I leave everything to the last minute, I feel pressured, and I can't perform like I want to...and that is my problem today. This story feels like it is rambling with no clear direction.

It will be August next week. I've been doing this crazy Uber-Mom thing for a little over a month now...and I'm getting kinda tired of it. I've done all the responsible and organized things that I know I am supposed to do! I write out my schedule for the week and make myself a to-do list. I plan my days down to the minute so that I can do what I need to do while getting my kids where they need to be.

Yet my laundry sits.

And I haven't done a real grocery shop in a long time.

We eat out pretty regularly.

And I haven't cooked a healthy meal once this week.

Why am I always feeling behind?

...because I'm not superhuman!! So what do I do? I think I have to begin by letting things go. Maybe I use "Drive Up and Go" for my groceries a little more regularly so that we have healthy food to eat for my family. And maybe I plan easy meals like I used to when I was working full-time out of the house...there's no shame in using the Crock Pot, even in the summertime!

I think I also might need to ask for help with things like the laundry and Ubering my kiddos. I know my family and other parents who have kids in the same activities will always be willing to take a load off me once in a while. And I can leave a basket of laundry for my husband or even my kids to fold while they watch TV.

But I really think that, most importantly, I need to tell myself it is OK if things aren't perfect…. That what I have been doing is good enough. I also need to remind myself that there is no problem with taking a break when I need it. Maybe a little brain check-out in front of reality television will give me the boost that I need to keep going.

Lastly, I need to remember that this Uber-Mom life won't last forever. There will come a time when my kids will come and go and won't need me as much…and I'll miss it. This time that I have with my kids, whether it is in the car or over take-out at our family table, is worth every second.

So, what will August look like? Probably the same mayhem that July gave me…but with a little more lightheartedness, grace, and gratitude! Cheers to that!

CHAPTER 22

it doesn't have to be this way

IT HAS BEEN A BUSY WEEK. I HAVE BEEN PULLED IN about twenty-five different directions, with pretty much every part of my day planned down to the minute. I was looking forward to today. It was the one day of the week when my schedule was light. I *finally* had time to sit and write…one of my favorite things to do.

I had planned a relaxing morning all for myself. I woke up early before my family and did a nice workout as I watched the sunrise. I got everyone up, prepared breakfast, and even took a minute to watch out the window as my kids walked down the street to the bus stop. I very rarely have time to watch them when they know I'm not looking. I don't know why I love to do that sometimes…. I enjoy getting a glimpse of them in their "natural habitat."

I poured myself a nice cup of coffee and went to take a shower before I sat down to begin my work day. While I was getting ready for my shower, I heard voices downstairs. So I went to check it out.

I found a friend of mine visibly shaking, on the verge of tears, and my husband talking on the phone with my son (whom I had just watched walk to the bus stop).

What was going on?

An active shooter alarm had just gone off at our local high school. My friend, also a teacher there, heard the alarm, escaped from the building and came home. Both she and my husband were trying to get a hold of the kids on the bus to tell the bus driver NOT to go to the high school and drop off the kids. My husband was talking to my son, a freshman at the school, about the active shooter.

I immediately got a text from my daughter, who, despite being a middle school student, rode the same bus with high schoolers. She texted, "Is everything OK? What's going on?"

I got on the phone with her to tell her that things weren't safe at the high school and to help get the bus driver to stop the bus. My son was on it, bravely standing up, telling the driver what he knew, and asking her to stop the bus.

I was in shock.
My kids were confused.
My friend was scared.

All I could do was hug my friend and wait. I knew my kids were OK. I knew that the entire bus of kids they were riding with wasn't going to walk into danger.

But worry set in.
Was everyone at school OK?
I wanted to cry, but I couldn't.
I felt stuck.
I felt numb.

I just wouldn't let my brain imagine what was happening inside the high school at that moment.

Although it felt like a lot longer, I think it was only a few minutes that passed with all of these big, unpleasant, and high-energy emotions running through me. I immediately felt relief when, on the phone with the kids, I heard the bus driver announce that the active shooter alarm was not real.

It was a false alarm.

When we got confirmation a few moments later through email that an alarm had accidentally been triggered, I felt relief wash through me.

No one with a gun was hunting children in our local school.

Every single person involved in today's incident was OK.

But my friend was still shaking, and now she had to go back to school and go on with her day. The kids who were at school early that morning for AP testing had to put their feelings aside so they could do their best. My kids had to walk into that school with a new understanding that *this could happen to them at any time*. And even though I'm sure they already knew, it became very real to them... and to me....

False alarm or not.

I feel like active shooting tragedies happen daily around the world. I don't watch the news anymore because I just can't bear to see it. Every time I watch these tragedies and heartbreaks unfold on TV, it becomes too real. It feeds my fears, and I just won't allow that to happen. So now I choose what I want to read, not watch. I'm not putting on blinders...I'm just choosing where I want to focus my energy, and I'd rather read my news than watch it happen before my eyes. It is the exact reason why I'd rather not watch scary movies.

But I am well aware of every single school shooting that has happened in the last twenty or more years since I've been in education. Back in 2000, when I started my career, I was only twenty-two years old. My first year of teaching was the first (and only) time I experienced a real lockdown.

I was in Los Angeles, California. Our classrooms were built in pairs and in separate buildings connected by an outdoor hallway. One morning, there was an active shooter in the neighborhood, and because most of our school "building" was outside, we were asked to lock the doors to our classrooms. There was no way for kids to use the bathroom. We didn't have any access to our lunches. And we were locked down from about 10 a.m. until 4 p.m. when they finally apprehended the active shooter.

Six hours with about fifty kids and two teachers. All of us were scared. We could hear helicopters, police cars, and gunshots. There was no way we were going to go on "business as usual" while all of that was going on outside our doors.

So, we got creative. We braided our hair. We ate the snacks and water that we all had in our classrooms in case of an earthquake. We played games, and we read books. We turned on music to drown out the sounds from around the neighborhood. And when we needed to use the bathroom, we set up boys' and girls' buckets in our closets to use if needed. We did our best to make this really awful situation feel "normal."

That's not OK.

It is not normal for teachers to lock their students with them in a classroom with active shooting happening outside their door.

When we were safe to leave, we were all escorted by police officers from the school grounds so that we felt assured that we were safe to get home. I remember the police officer asking me if I was OK. I honestly answered, "Yes" because I thought I was....

It wasn't until I pulled into my driveway that I started to shake. It was the shake of adrenaline leaving my body. I was holding it together all day for my students, and I didn't allow myself to admit that I was scared.

I was twenty-two years old, across the country from my family, and scared on the job.

It didn't have to be that way.

I cried a lot that night. I remember drawing myself a warm bath and bawling my eyes out. I was crying as a way to process my fear but also as a way to express my relief. I was OK. My students were OK. And the "bad guy" was gone.

I went through the rest of my time in that position, carrying a little bit of fear every time I stepped on campus.

Would it happen again?
Would I hear gunshots?
Would I have to lockdown again?

Fast forward twelve years later. In those twelve years, I taught health, third grade, fourth grade, and fifth grade in three other schools. I moved back home, got married, and was pregnant with my second child. A lot had changed!

About five years had passed between the Virginia Tech Massacre and now. I was sitting in an IEP meeting when an alert went off on my phone. There was an active shooter at a school in Connecticut called Sandy Hook Elementary School.

I was an elementary school teacher. And this was very real to me. I remembered how it felt to lockdown in Los Angeles twelve years prior. I was glued to the news, crying along with the families that were interviewed. And worrying that, once again, this became *way* too real for me…for the world.

This is not OK.
It doesn't have to be like this.

It took me ten years before I could read Scarlett Lewis's book called *Nurturing Healing Love*. She is an incredible woman who lost her son Jesse in the Sandy Hook school shooting. She now runs the "Choose Love Movement," which I follow very closely. She took her grief and turned it into something that her son would want everyone to do…to choose love rather than hate. And she's encouraging schools, educators, and students to do exactly that.

I am in awe of this woman, and I hope to meet her someday.

Through every single year that I taught in a public school classroom, we learned about lockdown drills. They changed several times as law enforcement learned about the best ways to save and protect lives through every school shooting tragedy the world experienced.

Every single year, I practiced with my young students what to do if someone was trying to kill us.

I locked the door.
I drew the shades.
I asked the kids to be quiet.
I listened to police in the hallway practicing with us, stomping their big boots and jiggling our doors loudly.

I told the kids to have something nearby to throw at an intruder if they got into our classroom somehow.

But you know what? The whole time, I knew perfectly well that I wouldn't sit in my classroom with these kids if I heard gunshots in the building. I would get the heck out of that building as fast as I could, and we would run.

I would tell the kids to run to the neighbors.
I would promise them I would do my best to get them to safety.
A promise that I wasn't totally sure I could keep.

Today, my friend did exactly that. She ran for her life, and she came to my house to be sure her child and my children were safe. She got the heck out of a building that she thought contained someone who would try to kill her.

Today, I felt helpless because I couldn't be totally sure that I could keep my kids safe. My children were on the way to a place that I thought contained someone who would try to kill them.

We were lucky. There wasn't an active shooter. It was a false alarm. I wouldn't be that person who was interviewed on the news, recounting the fear I felt for my kids and my community. I wouldn't attend funerals for teachers, friends, and students. My life hasn't changed forever.

We got an email shortly after the incident, assuring families that the school was safe and it was only a "false alarm." The email said:

There is no cause for concern.

But I do feel concerned. I feel concerned that we live in a world where we fear sending our kids to school. I have concerns that a life-changing alarm was accidentally triggered, sending kids, parents, and teachers into a justifiable panic. I feel concerned that I am being told not to feel concerned! But the email went on to say:

The incident occurred before the start of the school day, and there were very few students in the building.

Does it matter *how many* people experience this fear? Those few students, educators, and staff mean something! No matter how many people are involved, they are loved by parents, friends, grandparents, community members...and they matter! I feel concerned about that statement. And finally, the email ended with:

We anticipate the remainder of the day will proceed as normal.

As normal.

Those "few" students and faculty members were very shaken. My friend literally ran for her life. My kids felt scared when my husband and I called them to tell them that there was an active shooter at the high school.

There is nothing "normal" about that.

How about *we work to process the emotions* that we may be feeling about this "unfortunate incident?" I am lucky that I can sit here, write my story, and express my emotions.

....But my kids, my friend, and the rest of our local high school?

They were sitting in classrooms trying to teach and learn, no matter what transpired that morning. In my opinion, this was a traumatic experience, and it doesn't seem that anyone wants to help process that with our children and teachers. Life will just go on "as normal."

It doesn't have to be this way.

We need to do better for our kids, our families, and our communities. Imagine a world where we don't feel scared to send our kids to school. Imagine a world where we didn't have to make promises to our children and students that we aren't sure we can keep.

We need to teach the world that their emotions matter. We need to stop minimizing our unpleasant feelings...telling us that we *shouldn't* be concerned, and expressing that we just need to get back to normal. We have to stop telling each other not to feel. It isn't human. We are meant to feel pleasant emotions, and in order to feel them, we need to be given time to move through the unpleasant ones.

There is one thing that connects all of us, no matter where we were raised, our income, our heritage, or the color of our skin...and that is our emotions. We all feel angry at times. We all feel ashamed. We all feel scared. But we have to stop using our emotions as weapons and excuses for our behavior. And we need to stop dismissing our emotions so that we can "move on." Because I'll tell you what... none of us are moving on! And the actions in today's world are evidence of that.

None of this is "normal."

And it doesn't have to be this way.

CHAPTER 23

a follow up...with gratitude

IT IS UNUSUAL FOR ME TO WRITE TWO STORIES IN A week. But I feel like I have more to express and am compelled to follow up on my last story, "It Doesn't Have to Be This Way." So here goes:

> As many of you may or may not know,
> it happened again the next day.
> For real, this time.

It felt like a regular morning. My family woke up, we ate breakfast, we packed our things, and we all went our separate ways. The kids went to school, my husband settled into his home office, and I hit the road for work.

I was driving into the parking lot of my building when my phone started to light up. I pulled into a spot, put my car in park, and looked at my screen. I had so many texts and calls.

From a friend, "Something is happening at the high school."

From my son's school, "The high school has entered an unplanned lockdown."

From my husband, already in contact with my son, "Someone is on the soccer field with a weapon."

I think my heart dropped into my stomach. My breathing became fast and shallow. What was happening?

What do I do? I sat there frozen and stunned. Students were counting on me. I had to go to work. I felt like I was in a fog as I went through the motions...

I put on a smile.
I monitored my phone.
My son's school texted and emailed constant updates.
My husband was in contact with my son.
And there was nothing I could do other than...
trust,
not let my brain go to dark places,
and wait.

It felt like years before I saw the message I was praying for...that all was safe and secure at the high school. My son was on his way home from school early, safe and sound.

Texts were flying through my phone about what happened. But I didn't care about any of that stuff. All that was going through my mind was...

My son, his classmates, and his teachers were safe.
Today didn't turn out the way it could have.
And that is all that mattered.

My drive home was a blur. I couldn't wait to get home and see my son. The moment I set eyes on him...to say I felt relieved might be an understatement.

It's going to take me a while to process my feelings over all of this…my son locked in school while someone with a weapon stood outside, threatening his safety.

It's going to be a while before I move through the emotions I have about it all. But I'll tell you one feeling that I know clear as day.…

I feel so incredibly grateful.

First and foremost, I'm grateful the incident didn't escalate. To my knowledge, no one was physically harmed. Students and teachers went home safely to their families.

Second, I'm grateful to our local first responders. They knew exactly how to keep everyone inside that school and in our community safe. They were ready to risk their lives to protect our loved ones. They sat watch at all the schools to ensure security beyond the high school. And the School Resource Officer, after all he faced that morning, took the time to assure our kids that they were safe before making their way home to process it all with their families.

I'm also grateful to our school leaders. I know they are very well prepared for events exactly like this, but no one wants to imagine it happening on their watch. I'm grateful for the protocols they created and swiftly put into action. I don't envy their positions. A lot more than we realize rests on their shoulders. And I'm not sure we recognize that often enough.

Lastly, I am grateful to each and every educator and staff member who was inside the building that day. They were ready to protect our kids at any cost and kept everyone calm when they may have been feeling as scared, uncertain, and shaken as the children sitting in front of them. There are not enough words to describe how grateful I am for everything my son's teacher did for her students that day. She has superhero status in my mind. They all do.…

I'm not entirely sure I can label and manage every emotion I feel about what happened. I'll get there eventually. But in the meantime.…

I'm choosing to look for and appreciate the helpers.

Because if I look at anything else at this moment, I'll risk losing hope.

And it doesn't have to be that way.

CHAPTER 24

the worst!

MY DAUGHTER'S HAPPY PLACE IS IN MUSIC AND DANCing. She loves to sing and can often be found twirling in circles while belting out a tune. Sometimes, she even gets me to turn our everyday conversation into a musical. I'll ask her what she wants for breakfast, and she will sing to me that she wants cereal and a smoothie in a voice that sounds like it belongs in "Mary Poppins." To go along with it, I will often sing my reply back to her. We can go on and on like that for a while! It is so uniquely my daughter, and I love every minute of it. We create musicals about what to pack for trips, plan for meals, or even how the day went.

One day, I woke my daughter up for school, and she came downstairs for breakfast, looking a little down. To cheer her up, I prompted her to sing a musical with me. I asked her in a sing-songy voice, "What's the matter, my dear?"

Unhappily playing along, she sang back to me, "School sucks."

As a former public school educator and mom, that response made my heart hurt a little bit. All of us want our kids to *like* school.

We want them to learn, be excited about what they are learning, and be happy to go there every day.

Plus, school is a non-negotiable part of life. And since it is a necessity, it can be challenging for kids and parents when our children express how much they hate it...especially if they struggle in some area. When they struggle academically or socially, getting through a school day can be a real challenge, and that can be hard for kids to express.

While my daughter has expressed how hard school can be and her frustration over the amount of work she is given, I've never heard her use that language when it comes to going to school in the morning.

To play along, I kept singing with her. Back and forth, she told me what was hard about school, and I offered suggestions to help her. I listened to her singing and also sang my empathy back to her. We ended our duet with a hug, and she reluctantly walked out the door to catch the bus.

While I was grateful my daughter didn't have any difficulty articulating her feelings, my heart sank as I watched her walk down the street. I didn't want her to go to school feeling that way, but her emotions were valid; they mattered, and I needed to let her have them. But man! They weighed on me that morning.

I couldn't stop thinking about what she sang and expressed to me. Why did she hate school so much? Why do a lot of kids hate it? So I did some thinking and came to this conclusion...which honestly wasn't rocket science.

School is hard.

Being a former teacher, I have firsthand knowledge about education, and I think that helps me understand how rough school can be for kids. I also know how much time, energy, and dedication many teachers and other staff put into their work. While there are imperfections I see in the public education system, I am putting it out there that **I, in no way, blame anyone working with children for these faults.**

As a kid, I loved school (which is why I probably became a teacher!). I was always curious and wanted to learn as much as I could. I liked to play "school" with my friends and sister down in our basement. When my kids were young, I took them places where they could be curious and learn, too. And yet...neither of my kids really like school all that much. Both seem to be counting the days until it is over. Both the social pieces and the learning are hard.

> It is tough.
> Learning is hard.
> And school is all about academic and social learning.

I get why my daughter expresses her dislike about school. At times, she feels she spends all day trying to achieve something that feels unachievable. More often, she expresses that she has ZERO interest in learning what she's required to learn. That's a tough sell...I get it! She doesn't have AHDH or any sort of Learning Disability, but if she did, that would be an even harder sell.

The non-emotionally intelligent mom inside of me wanted to tell my daughter to "suck it up" when she told me through song that she didn't want to go to school that day. Sometimes, there's a part of me that has a hard time understanding my daughter's school experience. I loved school, so I was having a hard time grasping why she really didn't. But then I remembered....

Most kids spend thirteen years in school.

I tried to imagine having a job I hated and having to go there for thirteen years of forty-hour weeks, just like my daughter. This "ah-ha" moment made it easier for me to get rid of the "suck it up" attitude and take what my daughter was saying to me that morning a little more seriously.

I decided to write this story so I could think about the many conversations my daughter and I have had about this topic lately. I've been listening, and I wanted to reflect on what a school day really looks like for her so I could start to understand. I also thought about what I know about teaching in a classroom and have been listening to my friends who are still teaching in public schools. This has certainly helped my understanding grow....

So here's what I know, understand, and have reflected on about my daughter's frustration over school....

Like I said, school is hard. Kids need an extremely large amount of energy to get through it every day. Imagine, for a second, spending the entire day doing something that is really, really difficult for you.... For me, that is usually something tech-related. Now imagine doing that the next day and the day after that. Imagine doing that every day for an entire school year.

No, thank you.

But now imagine how much more energy it takes for a kid that may be struggling with something else...a mental health or social issue, ADHD, or learning disability. Those kiddos need to expend even MORE energy on each activity they come across at school. Imagine the mental and emotional energy kids use when they need help with something. For example, when class sizes are big, they have to wait for their teacher to finish working with a small group or another student. This can feel frustrating and requires a lot of emotional energy from a child to keep them from being dysregulated from waiting or overly anxious about how much time they will have left to complete their work.

Going to school sometimes requires more energy than students have to give!

Other than energy, schoolwork is hard, too! Public schools usually have fast-paced curricula that focus on breadth, not depth. Whether or not a student is interested doesn't matter.... If plant parts are taught in second grade, that's what they will learn! This can cause a lot of frustration for all students. A lack of interest means that a child is going to have to work extra hard to pay attention and get the work done.

In addition, mastery expectations may be too high. For example, expecting third graders to know how to multiply after a minimal amount of instruction is tough! Most children, but especially those with learning disabilities, usually need more time before information and processes truly click. Teachers face time constraints that require them to move forward, even if students need more work on a particular skill. Most kids could benefit from working at a personalized pace, not the pace determined by the school district or the state.

Critical thinking is important in public schools. However, a student needs to really understand a concept or needs to sufficiently process background information before they can critically think about a topic. However, when they are asked to do so regardless of their understanding, this level of difficulty may be too high for a student to reach, causing frustration.

On the other hand, if too much time is devoted to a topic or lesson, that can be even more boring or difficult, causing even more frustration. Although many teachers try to make their lessons engaging and interesting, some topics just aren't. And with most lessons scripted for public school teachers these days, some lessons are just really bad, aren't taught well, or are paced poorly. And let's face it, some topics aren't developmentally appropriate for many kids in the class.

Another issue that can make school challenging for kids is the number of distractions they must manage each day! I know that, as a teacher, I felt this stress. Classrooms, hallways, cafeterias, gyms, and even before/after school holding zones are usually noisy.

While teachers work hard to manage behavioral problems, they can be bothersome at best, and at worst, they can be very upsetting. Depending on the school's climate, there may be a lot of movement and behavior issues in public areas, bathrooms, and unstructured environments.

Public school classrooms have a lot of students in them. Attention from fellow students and school friends can feel overwhelming to kids, especially those who are easily distracted or overwhelmed. Visual distractions are also rampant in many public schools. While many teachers spend their own money to make the classrooms as soothing and calm as possible, sometimes children struggle with everything there is to look at around them. Sometimes, kids work much better with one or two people or in smaller rooms with calm environments.

For children who need quiet to concentrate, all of this sensory stimulation can be energy-draining. And for kids who are susceptible to sensory overload, this can cause burnout!

Organizational demands are another area in which students can become overwhelmed and frustrated. This is especially true in today's public school climate, where little to no time is devoted to objectives that are "unacademic," such as organization. Students have a variety of classes, with a matching notebook, folder, and papers to manage both at school and at home. They also usually have a computer of some kind to manage and remember to plug in and bring back and forth.

Therefore, frustration starts even before academics begin!

This can impact children when they get older in middle school and beyond. If a teen's teacher doesn't require a particular organization system, they may develop one themselves, which may or may not be successful. And, with a lot of options to organize materials and no school-wide organization system in place, children need to follow many different systems from all of their teachers, and this can also be greatly energy-sucking for kids.

While public schools, especially where my children attend, work hard to create community throughout the building, the students may not be feeling it. Feeling as if they belong, as though they are an important part of a group, makes a big difference in how children feel about school. Some kids may just not jive, no matter how hard the teacher or the school tries. More often than not, there are just some kids who like to exclude others.

This stinks, but it is true.

And I've seen it firsthand.

For some kids, a sense of community, or being part of a group, is the main reason they *like* going to school. And if there are problems between friends or a lot of drama, this can cause anxiety and sadness. It is also tough when children don't have any classes or lunch with their friends, so they feel isolated and alone. Kids want to feel as though they are around people who "get" them, but that isn't always an option, no matter how strong the school community may be.

So, with all of this and more...what do I do? How do I help my daughter adjust her feelings about school?

One thing I know I need to do is keep the dialogue going. I will try my best to be there when she gets home from school, give her a snack, and let her talk if she needs to. Sometimes, just listening is enough...I have to remember that I don't need to solve all the problems. She may just need to decompress.

Second, I need to make sure I communicate what is happening with school. Right now, she still willingly goes to school and isn't *always* saying she hates it. But if it ever gets to that point, I will certainly reach out to her teachers and her guidance counselor for advice on how she can be more supported at school.

Third, it is important for me to monitor my daughter's energy demands. When she comes home from school and appears to have nothing left in her tank for extra classes, activities, or even homework, then maybe I give her a pass that night. Or, we prioritize what we need to do and what we can skip out on.

Lastly, it is important that I help my daughter replenish her "energy bank." I can help her learn to identify activities, people, and habits that help her come alive. She adores music, drawing, and her quiet time. If she gets those three things every day, she can bounce back from the difficulties of school more easily. It will be important, especially through these tumultuous middle school years, to build that time into her day so she can counterbalance her school experience and build up her self-confidence. In the meantime, I will keep filling her emotional bucket by freely giving hugs and putting little notes and treats on her school lunch to let her know she is loved. Sometimes, the small things can have a big impact!

More than anything, I want my daughter to know that I am taking it seriously that she is saying she hates school. I know it doesn't mean she will *always* hate it or that she is going to drop out.

It simply means that one morning, at that moment when she sang it to me, she was having unpleasant feelings about school.

And it was important for her to know that I heard her frustration and that I understood.

If we were in a musical right now, I'd sing this out loud to her....
Somehow,
Some way,
You will ride this wave
And together,
We will get to the other side.

CHAPTER 25

where crisis can lead us

IT IS FUNNY HOW THINGS COME TO US WHEN WE NEED them the most....

Last week, I was working on a session with one of my students. We were talking about friendships and how they can be full of ups and downs. I often read books with my students to promote discussion. Together, we were reading a chapter full of tips about how to manage and navigate working things out when there is a disagreement with a friend. The chapter began by showing us the Chinese word for crisis. This word could describe the way the world is at this moment. I found this interesting because it reminded me that John F. Kennedy once inspired his country by saying,

"The Chinese use two brush strokes for the word *crisis*. One brush stroke stands for danger; the other for opportunity. In a crisis, beware of danger—but recognize the opportunity."

After my session, the chapter I read and JFK's quote, it got me thinking. What is a 'crisis,' exactly? I think it depends....

For a school-aged child, a crisis could most certainly be an argument with a friend.
For middle schoolers, a crisis could occur when they're on the receiving end of a mean comment.
For high schoolers, a crisis could feel like a rejection from a college of choice.
For adults, crises could be everywhere!
For the world, it could mean conflict and destruction.

Crises can be heartbreaking, life-changing, and overwhelming. They can bring us to our knees and evoke a slew of emotions. We can have a mid-life crisis, a natural disaster, violence, confrontation...it gets pretty bleak when you really start thinking about it.

My student and I were discussing a particular incident with one of her friends on the playground. This friend was not nice to her, putting their relationship in crisis. We began talking about how to respond in the best way possible.

We talked about how a smaller problem can turn into a big one really quickly, depending on the response. The best way to turn a little problem into a big one is to stew about it, not talk about it, or talk about it to everyone else BUT the person you need to speak with, and then eventually blow up.

I made sure this student understood that it is absolutely OK and natural to get angry when someone is unkind. We talked about ways to manage the anger before saying or doing something in retaliation that can't be taken back, making the initial problem much worse.

The biggest lesson I wanted my student to take away is this...*in every crisis, there IS an opportunity, as well as a choice.* In this situation, my student had the choice to end the friendship and find an opportunity to make new friends with whom they better connected.

Or, they could work it out and maybe find the opportunity to grow their friendship bond and make it even stronger.

After this lesson with my student, I did some research and learned that JFK was a little inaccurate about the meaning of the brush strokes in the Chinese word for 'crisis.' According to CEO and author Emily Chang, the first character of the word crisis in Chinese does, in fact, translate to "danger." However, the second character by itself doesn't really translate to opportunity. By itself, the word more likely means "a crucial point when things begin to change." In other words, the Chinese brush strokes for crisis most likely translate to "a turning point + danger."

So what does this mean for my lesson to my student and the message I'm trying to tell you in this story?

For a school-aged or middle school student fighting with a friend, a mean remark can be the turning point they both need to either end the friendship or work things through.

For a high schooler who didn't get into the college of their choice, this moment could be a turning point for them to go in a different direction...one they didn't expect but could be exactly what they need.

For adults who face heartbreaking crises, we may realize that there are many elements at play. It could leave us at a crossroads where things could go in a variety of directions. The question is... what do we do?

For my student, this might look like taking a moment to process the anger she feels with breathing tools, doing an activity that clears her head, writing her feelings down, talking to a trusted adult, and deciding if the situation is worth fighting about.

For high schoolers, this might also look like taking a moment to process the disappointment of the rejection letter from the college of their dreams and then deciding on other options.

For adults, my answer to this question goes back to JFK's wisdom.

In a crisis, it is important for us to remain aware of the danger and do everything we can to get a positive outcome for ourselves.

I am not Chinese, and I don't have much knowledge of the Chinese written language. My research about the Chinese word for a crisis could be entirely inaccurate, and I welcome someone knowledgable to teach me more. However, I do know that our perspective on our lives plays a HUGE part in how we want to respond to the challenges life throws us.

The key message from what I'm trying to say is that I believe *it is our choice whether to focus on the obstacle or the opportunity in any given situation.*

Imagine if the school-aged child sees the opportunity to express her feelings and talk it out with the friend that hurt her.

Imagine if the high schooler sees the opportunity to explore somewhere new that they hadn't imagined before.

Imagine if the adult was able to share their experience with a traumatic event in order to help others going through something similar.

These are the kinds of opportunities and turning points that a crisis can lead us toward. What kind of world would we live in if we could end the fighting, stop saying things we can't take back, and work together to better each other? We can either say it will never happen, simply imagine it will, or create an amazing world for each other...the choice is always there!

CHAPTER 26

overthinkers anonymous

HI. MY NAME IS JENNY. AND I THINK I MIGHT BE AN overthinker. I've been told that a few times.

Or maybe I worry that I think about things too much.

I think I'm just good at self-reflecting.

I'm a Libra, so I like to keep everything in balance, and I spend a lot of time thinking about how to do that.

I care about people, and I am always thinking about others.

I'm good at reading people and showing empathy.

I am always thinking about how I can be helpful to others.

But that doesn't make me an overthinker, does it?

Maybe it does. I don't know....

Is being an overthinker **bad**?

Oh boy...I might have a problem.

The other day, I saw a friend I hadn't seen in a while. It was good to see her and give her a hug. But when I looked at her, I saw something in her eyes and heard her take a big, deep sigh. And I said something out loud that I was thinking....

"You look tired."

Don't get me wrong. My friend is drop-dead gorgeous. Even on her most tired days, she remains beautiful. But I got the feeling that I insulted her with my words. And I went home, trying to figure out how I could tell her that I didn't mean to hurt her feelings.

So I texted her and told her exactly what I just told you. I wanted her to know that it was good to see her and that I wish I had been more thoughtful in the first few things I said to her.

Sensing that I was a little worried about insulting her, she addressed me as her "fellow overthinker" and pretty much told me there was no need to apologize. She wasn't hurt by my words. This wasn't the first time I've been told I overthink things. In fact, I **know** I can do this sometimes.

And then...you guessed it...I started to overthink that!

And if you know anything about me, when I am overthinking, I tend to do some research about different topics that come up for me from time to time. So, I dove into some reading about what overthinking is and what to do about it. My friend told me I wasn't the only one...that I have fellow overthinkers out there! Perhaps a few of them are reading this right now!

Here's what I learned....

According to Forbes Health, research suggests that seventy-three percent of twenty-five to thirty-five-year-olds chronically overthink, along with fifty-two percent of people ages forty-five to fifty-five.

Yup...that's me!

And there is some evidence out there that suggests that women are more likely to be overthinkers than men.

Huh...whelp! That's me again.

But honestly, after all my research, I learned that no matter your age or the gender in which you identify, everyone overthinks sometimes. I learned that overthinking comes in two forms: ruminating about the past and worrying about the future.

Don't confuse this with problem-solving. When someone problem-solves, they think about a solution.

Don't confuse overthinking with self-reflection, either. Healthy self-reflection is learning new things about oneself or gaining a new perspective on a situation. Self-reflection serves a purpose.

In contrast, overthinking is simply dwelling on a problem, noticing how bad we feel, and thinking about all the things we have no control over. Overthinking about a problem doesn't help develop new insight.

Through my research, I came to a real "ah-ha" moment about problem-solving, self-reflection, and overthinking…it isn't about the time we spend in our thoughts. When we spend time thinking about creative solutions or learning from our behavior, it is productive.

But time spent overthinking, no matter how much or how little, isn't life-enhancing.

The challenging thing about overthinking is that our brains can trick us into believing that worrying and ruminating are somehow helpful. Sometimes, overthinking can lead us to believe that it can prevent something bad from happening, and if we don't worry enough or rehash the past enough, then somehow, we will encounter more problems.

The research is pretty clear…overthinking is not healthy and will not prevent or solve problems. There are links to overthinking and other mental health problems like depression and anxiety. It is likely that overthinking causes mental health decline. And the more our mental health declines, the more we overthink. It can be a vicious downward spiral that is hard for us to recognize when we are caught in the middle of it.

This pause to do my research helped me to transition my brain and to be sure that my thoughts were more on the helpful self-reflecting and problem-solving side. My friend's call out of my behavior got me to notice that I was….

Reliving an embarrassing moment in my head repeatedly.

Spending time thinking about the hidden meaning in our interaction.

Rehashing the conversation I had with my friend and thinking about all the things I wished I had or hadn't said.

Constantly reliving my mistake.

Replaying the interaction in my mind.

And all of this background noise going on inside of my head was me allowing my brain to go into overthinking mode. The first step I needed to take was noticing and recognizing that my thoughts were starting to get carried away.

The second step I took was to pick a tool or two that could help me make a change in my behavior and reclaim my time, energy, and brain power. This is where this story comes in…it is a "mind dump" of sorts. Right now, I am using a tool that I know well! When I ruminate and worry, I get it all out of my head by writing my thoughts down on paper. This tool literally drains my brain of all the thoughts that aren't serving me.

But before writing all of this down, I realized I needed to get out of my head and into my body. This is another tool for managing the thoughts in my mind that don't serve me. I simply stop what I am doing and notice my breathing. It is something I do many times before meditating. I feel the air going in and out of my nose. I feel my body in the chair or my feet on the ground. Sometimes, I connect with my body by dancing around to music or even doing some exercise. It all depends on what I have time for and what kind of connection to myself I feel like I need.

And if I really crave it and have the time for it, I get outside. One study done by the National Academy of Sciences of the United States of America shows that taking time in a nature-filled environment can decrease one's inclination toward rumination. Maybe it is the lack of noise and distractions out there in nature that does it for me. Or maybe it is the fact that being in nature allows me to focus on something larger than myself. But whatever the reason, I know that time in the fresh air helps me to shift my brain.

So, I did what I needed to do.

My friend helped me realize I was getting myself caught up in my own "stinking thinking." I picked a few tools to help my brain shift to thoughts that served me better than my overthinking. And I moved through it.

Am I still worried that I hurt my friend's feelings? Maybe.

Do I wish I said something different to my friend? Yes.

So, the third step I took was working to reframe my thinking. How could I rearrange these unhelpful thoughts into something that served me better? Reframing means looking for evidence that my emotions are clouding the reality of the situation and trying to see everything in a different way.

So, I did just that. I began to realize that there was nothing I could do to reverse time and go back to that exact moment with my friend. Her text was evidence to show me that I didn't hurt her feelings, and if I did, she forgave me before I was able to forgive myself. After reframing my unhelpful thoughts, gratitude sunk in, and I told myself that I am so thankful for friends like this in my life. I was also able to think....

I am good at self-reflection.

I am good at balancing all that life throws at me.

I am a good person that thinks about others and shows empathy.

With this new reframe of my thoughts, I was able to see that my friend did me a favor. She got me to really think about if I am overthinking, problem-solving, and/or self-reflecting. **This whole time, I've identified myself as an overthinker, but maybe I'm not.** I think I was right about myself in the first place. I may spend a lot of time thinking, but that time is insightful. I often self-reflect and solve problems! This realization was such a relief to me, and I couldn't have done it without using the emotion regulation tools I know and love.

So, if any of this resonates with you, you belong here with me! Let's blow this Overthinkers Anonymous meeting and identify ourselves as something more! Perhaps we can start the "Thoughtful Humans Club?" Let's do it!

Say it with me:

"Hi, my name is _____, and I'm a thoughtful human."

CHAPTER 27

perfectly imperfect

WHEN I PRESENT WELLNESS WORKSHOPS FOR EDUCAtors and staff, I share a slide that lists a lot of things about me. It is meant to explain a little bit about my background, my certifications, and my interests. However, one thing I intentionally listed on this descriptive slide about myself is the word "imperfect."

As much as I try to model emotion regulation and mindfulness…I am not always perfect. I have moments of ignoring my body's signals that I am feeling something big, letting the emotional side of my brain take over, and reacting in a way that I'm not proud of.

When I share things like this about myself with others, I want to make the point that just because we have all the tools in the world to make us successful, it doesn't mean we always use them properly. I want others to hear that mistakes happen, even to the best of us, and that is OK. *It is how you learn from the mistakes that matters the most.*

The story that I am writing about today happened roughly four years ago. It feels very vulnerable to share because it is not one of my finest moments. And as a teacher, a mom, and a social-emotional learning coach, it is downright embarrassing.

Let me explain....

I've had more than several clear moments of emotional regulation failure in my adult life. One moment that I can really pinpoint comes from the time when COVID first hit.

This was a really hard time for me. I was teaching third grade, and our district decided to quickly switch to distance learning with our students. I was using Zoom for the first time and working from home without the direct support of my colleagues that I'd always been accustomed to. I was trying to manage not only my students and this new change in routine but my family as well. I couldn't see my extended family or friends. My house suddenly felt much smaller, and there were so many unknowns about what was to come.

Thinking back on that time, I know I am not alone when I say that I was struggling to figure it all out. I just couldn't wrap my mind around what was happening with this virus. I wasn't used to feeling so separate and fearful of the rest of the world. Even though I tried really hard to use my positive thinking skills and look for opportunities in all of the obstacles I was facing, I had too many moments of feeling isolated, worried, anxious, exhausted, and overwhelmed (to say the least).

I remember March 13, 2020, very clearly. COVID sent my school home that Friday—uncertain if we would be returning after the weekend. We had no idea that we wouldn't go back to our classrooms at all that school year.

This was three days before my daughter's eighth birthday. Fearing that the mall would close, my daughter and I went out the next day to get her ears pierced, the biggest gift she asked for that year. Thankfully, we did because the next day, we were told that everything was closing...schools, restaurants, stores! You name it. We were all asked to stay home and stay safe. As a result, my daughter's birthday party for her family and friends was canceled. We couldn't go out to dinner to celebrate. We had to celebrate in our own way, at home, with the four of us.

My daughter enjoyed her birthday that year despite the fact that it was hard for her to understand why she couldn't be with everyone who loved her. Family and friends brought her gifts, leaving them on our doorstep and waving from the window. We were able to order takeout from her favorite restaurant, and I made her a cake. We celebrated and did our best. But I felt for my daughter...for both of our kids. At times, this uncertainty was too much to bear!

As the months of isolation went on, our neighbors eventually figured out how to make the best of celebrating birthdays and other special occasions. I started to find joy in the creative ways that people were giving love to each other despite the disconnection and isolation. The most common way that my community celebrated birthdays for kids was with something I call "drive-bys."

Families bought giant signs and balloons to decorate the front of their houses and lawns. They made arrangements for everyone they knew to drive by their house, hand out a gift from their car window, and make as much noise as possible from the confines of their cars. The birthday kids often dressed up and stood in their driveway with their families, waving as their friends and loved ones passed by. I loved these celebrations! To see others' smiles was contagious. It gave my family a moment to connect with others and do something kind for someone else. I felt happy to see the community come together in a way that was socially distanced but, at the same time, celebratory.

I wished we had that idea for my daughter when her birthday came at the start of COVID. She missed out on that. But honestly, all kids were missing out on a lot of regular life things, and it was taking a toll on them. I saw that with my own children. And it left me worried about all the kids I knew...my students, our neighbors, and my family.

My roles as a teacher and parent of young kids made me feel very protective of children during that time. COVID was hard for adults to understand, let alone children. I felt like it was important that we do these drive-by birthday parties for our kids, despite the raucous it briefly caused in the neighborhood and the traffic jams that were created as a result on the streets. Besides, there was nothing else to do! We needed to find bits of joy in any way that we could!

But then there was that one day...I don't know what happened to me. All I know is that my emotions got the best of me, and I didn't handle myself in a way that made me feel proud.

A friend of mine arranged a birthday drive-by party for her daughter. Everyone that was invited planned to meet at a nearby parking lot of a local store. Once we all met together, the plan was to drive down the street to her house and honk our horns really loudly as we drove by the birthday girl. My kids were excited to blast "Birthday" by The Beatles from my car's speakers as we passed through the line of cars. It was fun to see everyone's excitement as they arrived at the arranged meeting place.

The mood changed when suddenly a store owner came out to the parking lot. She curtly asked us all to move because we were taking away parking spots for her customers who were coming to pick up items from her store. She didn't want to hear that we would only be there a short while and were just about ready to be on our way. She didn't care that we were gathering to brighten the day for one of our neighborhood kids. Her tone was rude, short, and combative. It soured the pleasant feelings that everyone had waited all day to spread for our friend.

In the past, before this event, I had a few harsh experiences with this woman. As a result, her behavior that afternoon triggered me. My feelings instantly went from pleasant to unpleasant, and I reacted to her without noticing or even taking a pause to recognize how I was feeling. It felt as if every emotion I was carrying about COVID came out in that instant. I was rude, short, and combative, directly back at her. I vowed right then and there that I would **never** step foot in her store again. This was the last straw!

But I didn't stop there. My angry energy was so high that I went home and wrote a nasty review on her Google page. A few hours later, I noticed it was taken down. This just made my anger turn to fury over the fact that she wasn't allowing honest reviews on her site. To spite her, I spent the next few days telling everyone I knew about my experience.

She read my review and knew I was unhappy. But she retaliated in anger back at me. She called the school department, demanding that I stop talking and posting reviews about her. She threatened the school department to stop me, or she would make sure she would tarnish my reputation as an educator.

After hearing this from my administration, I agreed that this woman wasn't worth it. For many reasons, I still believe that this woman made a lot of mistakes with me throughout the years. I will never give her business again. And I can still feel the visceral response of my anger in my core when I think about her or even drive by her building or into that parking lot.

However, when I think back on it, I know I was not perfect in the situation either. I reacted to my emotions and was unkind to her. I know that responding that way didn't serve me, her, or anyone around us.

If I could go back, I would change so many things about my reaction. I would do exactly what I teach others to do as a social-emotional learning coach and try to instill in my children:

Take a pause by taking a breath.
Notice sensations in your body.
Try to name how you're feeling.
Decide how to best respond with your integrity intact.

If I had done all of this, I probably would have noticed my breath and heartbeat quickening. I would have been able to label that I was feeling angry. I would have focused more on the joy I was trying to spread to my friend's daughter rather than the cranky woman standing in front of me. I would have told myself that fighting this woman wasn't worth the time or energy. I would have gotten in my car, driven through the birthday party, and gone home to focus my energy on the people and things that matter most to me.

But as they say, hindsight is 20/20. It is so easy for me to judge my actions. To say,

I was not being a good role model for my kids.
I was being a bully, just like her.
I failed at that moment.
How could I do such a thing?
I know better....

However, I also try to teach my students to be curious rather than judgemental. When mistakes happen, it is an opportunity to learn. I even give my students positive thoughts to pick from every day, and one of them says:

"FAIL = First Attempt In Learning."

So....four years later, as I write this story, I am finally asking myself, what happened, and what can I learn from it?

What happened is that I ignored everything I knew about good emotional regulation. I let my emotions cloud my rational thought. But more importantly, COVID happened. It was a rough time. And I wasn't thinking about what the woman who confronted me also may be going through.

I think times like these are good reminders to slow down. Emotional regulation isn't something humans are born with. We need to learn these things and practice them. We need to experience all the emotions, pleasant and unpleasant, in order to figure out the tools we need to regulate them. COVID tested each and every one of my tools. It gave me big opportunities to experience many different emotions at the same time. But it also allowed me to learn how to give myself grace.

I know and need to remember that grace can give me the strength to overcome any obstacle.

To be clear, none of us are perfect. We are going to make mistakes. We are going to hurt people and be hurt by others. We are going to feel big emotions that leave us with choices on how we want to respond. That includes you, me, *and* cranky shop owners. This is part of being human, right?

Reflecting on this imperfect moment in my life has given me the opportunity to help me grow. I know there will be other chances in my life to choose how I want to respond to someone who pushes my buttons. Hopefully, next time, I will respond in a way that will make me feel a little more proud of myself. And even better, I hope I will respond in a way that will also give my button pusher the gift I am giving myself right now…a simple five-letter word I think we can all benefit from:

Grace.

CHAPTER 28

you're a mean one, mr. grinch

AT THE MOMENT, I AM FEELING PRETTY DARN CHA-grined and embarrassed. I can't believe I could be so foolish! I read about these things all the time...people who get suckered into some sort of scam. When I read the stories, I often think to myself, "Really? Why did you go and give all your personal information to someone over the phone??" There is so much out there that tells you NOT to do that....why do people still do it? I often feel for the elderly because they are the ones that are targeted most often. But nope...this time, it was me.

On Sunday evening after Thanksgiving, my husband and I were relaxing on the couch, watching a cheesy Hallmark Christmas Movie. Andrew is so good at humoring me by watching these! Sometimes, I wonder if he actually enjoys these simple and predictable holiday romance flicks. Anyway, around 9 p.m., my mobile phone rang. When I checked the caller ID, I saw it was my bank, so I answered. The gentleman (more like "The Grinch") on the other end of the phone explained that my bank account had been hacked through my mobile app. He went into details about the name of the person who did this, how much they took (over $700!), and even the type of phone that accessed my app. I immediately shared that I didn't authorize this transaction. While on the phone, the man sent me an email from my bank that looked legitimate. Contained in the email was a link to click so I could regain control of my app again. I clicked the link and continued to hold for about a half hour, waiting for confirmation that my account was safe. However, we suddenly got disconnected.

I called the bank back and spoke to someone else. They explained that the wait time to speak with anyone would be over two hours, but he believed my account was hacked and the original phone call was fake. At first, I was in shock over this because I was actually talking on the exact phone number that called me in the first place. However, he explained that hackers often impersonate phone numbers. The bank froze all my accounts, and the man on the phone instructed me to call back when the wait time wasn't so long.

The next morning, I woke up and spoke to someone else from my bank. They confirmed that the original phone call was fraudulent but that she and her superior had never seen anything like it! I didn't give out any personal information. I simply clicked on a link they gave me, and while I was on hold, they proceeded to clear both my checking and my savings accounts! They did this all by mirroring my phone!

This very nice woman on the other end of the line walked me through resetting all of my accounts. When I was able to log back in, I saw that the thieves left me $2.07! How nice of them...like the Grinch stealing all of my presents and holiday decorations, leaving me with a few scattered and broken ornaments that fell off my tree on their way out the door! I felt so stressed and embarrassed. How could I let someone do this? I had thoughts running through my mind like...

You're so stupid.
Only morons do things like this.

The world is full of mean people.
I am never doing anything online or with my phone again.
How could you be such an idiot?

I felt deflated. I also felt violated and vulnerable. I thought back to the nice woman I spoke with on the phone. When I expressed that I felt dumb that I let this happen, she took a moment to tell me that it wasn't necessary for me to feel that way...that this type of theft was a new scam and even she had never seen it before. She soothed me by telling me, "don't be too hard on yourself. This honestly could have happened to anyone. This is not your fault." Her tone of voice and her words made me feel empowered and relieved. She was right...

I am not stupid.
Anyone could have made this mistake.
The world is full of mean people, but there are twice as many good people out there.
This mistake has made me that much more informed about doing things online and with my phone for the future.
How can I be even more smart about things like this moving forward?

And moving forward is exactly what I have to do. Sometimes, we come across situations in life that violate us, make us feel vulnerable, and even get us to blame ourselves for it! This person broke the law. This "grinch," we'll call him, stole from me. I am the victim. Since when are victims told that they are stupid, idiotic humans who deserve this kind of treatment because they asked for it? The woman I spoke with on the phone understood this and helped me see that I was not the problem in this situation. She simply reminded me that this is not my fault. It made me think about how many *other* times I blame myself for something that is out of my control and not my doing....

Now that I am sitting here thinking about it, there are plenty of times when this happens. When someone does something unkind towards me, I often wonder, "did I do something wrong?" This bank fraud situation made me realize that I need to stop doing this...my hacked account had nothing to do with me. This grinch stole from me. I didn't ask for it. I didn't invite them to steal from me. I trusted that this person had good intentions and that he was there to help me. That's what bad guys do...they prey on your trust.

Past-Jenny may have lost a little bit of trust in herself and humanity, leaving scars. But present-Jenny realizes that she can still trust. I just need to do it with my eyes a little more open. I need to remember that there are more "Whos" in this world than "Grinches" and that I can still trust that many people have good intentions out there. And one thing I need to stop doing is blaming myself for others' betrayals.

To the man who made me trust him and believe that he was trying to save me from fraud while simultaneously stealing from me, I want to say, "You're a mean one, Mr. Grinch." As Dr. Seuss says,

> "The three words that best describe you are as follows, and I quote: Stink, Stank, Stunk!"

And while I know that my Grinch won't return all the goods and I won't invite him to my Christmas dinner, I do forgive him. Because forgiveness allows me to let go of the connection I have with this man that wronged me and move forward, with or without them! I will channel my inner Cindy Lou Who and not let this mishap wreck my holiday spirit!

CHAPTER 29

looking for glimmers

I LOST TWO FRIENDS A LITTLE WHILE AGO...TWO GORgeous women in the prime of their lives left this world only a few months apart. The deaths of these friends left me devastated. It is hard for me to find the words to describe the feelings I had about it all...grief seems too simple.

I keep pictures of my friends near my desk so that I can see them smiling at me when I need it the most. I like to try to keep their memory alive in my brain, afraid that over time, I will forget something about them...their laughs, especially.

Even to this day, I often look for little signs that my friends are still with me even though I know they're gone. I think this is pretty common to do. I look for...

little white feathers,
thoughts in my mind that sound like they are talking to me,
ironic incidents that I like to imagine they orchestrated for me,
dreams of time spent with them,

...anything that tells me they are still there, supporting me, laughing with (or at!) me, and being my friend. Every once in a while, something happens, or I see something that stops me in my tracks because it reminds me of my friends. At first, it would make me feel sad, and I'd cry. But now, I may feel sadness, but it is mixed with something that makes me smile because I feel like sometimes these things happen to remind me that they are still here, guiding me somehow.

Some people like to call these things "signs." I call these moments "glimmers." They give me hope that my friends are somewhere happy and safe. And, although I feel a bit melancholy over a glimmer or two, I know that I am safe beyond the place in which I am dwelling. Sometimes, it feels like these glimmers come to me when I need it the most, leaving me feeling a little relieved to be reminded that everything is going to be OK.

In all honesty, we can find evidence for anything we want in this world. The other day, my daughter woke up and admittedly felt a bit grumpy. She didn't want to get out of bed, and when she did, she stubbed her toe. Then, she couldn't get her hair the way she wanted, leaving her late to catch the bus. On her way out the door, she declared, "This day is going to suck." When I asked her why, she listed all the horrible things that happened even before her day really started, and she was convinced more was going to come throughout the day.

She was probably right! I was willing to bet that one of her teachers or friends would be cranky, leaving my daughter feeling like she may be to blame. I was also guessing she wouldn't sit near the friend of her dreams at lunchtime, or she wouldn't like the food that was served to her. And, it was possible that she would leave something she needed in her locker and couldn't go get it while she was in class. **Something** was bound to happen throughout her school day that wasn't going to go her way, leaving her feeling like she had a bad day.

But the thing is, while she may be busy looking for all the things that weren't going her way during her day, she could possibly miss out on seeing all the things that were going right. I was willing to bet that one of her friends or teachers would help her with something. I was also guessing she would sit next to someone she enjoyed hanging out with at lunchtime, or she would be excited to see that I put a few Starbursts in the front pocket of her lunchbox. And, it was possible that even though she may have left something she needed in her locker, a classmate would have shared what she needed with her. **Something** was bound to happen throughout the day that acted as a glimmer, leaving her feeling like maybe the day wasn't so bad after all.

It all depends on what you choose to look for, right?
Glimmers.

I remember when 9/11 happened. Like many of you, I remember exactly where I was when the towers fell. And I remember the fear...a new fear that I never knew existed...came over me. I had trouble sleeping because I was so worried about the state of our world. The images I saw on TV haunted me. And then someone covering the news one night repeated a quote from Mister Rogers...something that seems to come back every time there's a major tragedy:

> "When I was a boy and I would see scary things in the news, my mother would say to me, 'Look for the helpers. You will always find people who are helping.'"

In anything, whether it is a major tragedy, the death of a friend, or worry that it will be a bad day, it is possible to find evidence to confirm any thought or feeling we may have. We can find the bad people, the things that went wrong, and the people to blame. But we can also find the good people, the things that went right, and the people who are trying to help. In other words, we can find the glimmers... the things that remind us that even though whatever is happening is scary, sad, frustrating, or overwhelming at the moment...we will get through it somehow. And it will be OK...eventually.

I had coffee with a friend the other day. It was a grim topic, but the conversation turned to my friend's concerns about social media and human trafficking. She informed me about some scary things that I wasn't aware of until this conversation. She said that, especially through COVID, when she was isolated in her home, she read a lot about this topic and learned more than she wanted to know. It left her feeling very concerned and fearful for young children in her world. So, she decided to take her fears and turn them into action. She made it her mission to walk every day and encouraged her friends to do the same to help spread awareness about this issue of human trafficking. But now, a few years later, she is still feeling discouraged that this issue is still very, very real.

I felt her frustration and despair. But then I told her that there is so much information out there about this topic.... I remember seeing what she was doing on social media a few years ago, informing her friends and loved ones about the issues around human trafficking. I've listened to stories on NPR and have read about what our government leaders are trying to do to stop online child predators. And while it can feel that **nothing** is changing and the issue is still a HUGE problem, there are a lot of people like her trying to raise awareness and make big changes. It is just taking a lot longer than expected. Instead of focusing on what *isn't* happening, I encouraged her to look for evidence that things are changing for the better.

Glimmers.

Evidence is all around us. Evidence that things are **bad**. Evidence that things are *changing for the better.* I guess it is a choice of what we want to focus on. I'm not saying we should ignore the things that we don't want to see...that isn't going to get us anywhere. But when those things are weighing on me so much that I can't seem to get out of the emotional wave that feels like it is drowning me, I don't always have a choice. Looking for glimmers is **one tool** that I use to help me stay afloat when the big emotional waves hit.

There are always glimmers for us to find.
We just have to have the courage to look.
What can you find today?

CHAPTER 30

emotions are my jam

EVER SINCE I TOOK MY FIRST RULER COURSE WITH Marc Brackett at the Yale Center for Emotional Intelligence, I really felt inspired to become what he calls "an emotion scientist." I have been tasked to work on increasing my emotion vocabulary and to really get curious about what I am feeling and why. I have worked with countless students, families, and educators about noticing the emotions they feel every day.

It sounds like a no-brainer, but I have learned and experienced that there are emotions behind everything in life. Our feelings drive things like motivation and decisions...you name it, there's an emotion there! Being an emotional scientist means that I try to look at my emotions as a guide towards the best responses for getting what I need.

The hardest part for most people, including myself, is recognizing that the things I tell myself and the actions that I take, those that serve me and those that don't, usually happen because I am feeling something big. I can be so disassociated that sometimes I am already knee-deep in negative self-talk or poor choices to see that there are several emotions swirling around inside of me.

I think most of us can say that we didn't grow up at a time when we learned how to understand emotions. My teachers didn't sit me down in elementary school and ask me how I was feeling. I didn't label my feelings on a Mood Meter. I wasn't taught tools to help me regulate my emotions. Sometimes, I had to figure it out on my own, and many times, the "tools" I created for myself weren't all that helpful. Othertimes, I had no idea what to do with everything that was going on inside of me. I chose actions, some helpful and some not, based on what made me feel the safest. But the craziest part for me to explain to others is that even though I teach this stuff, I still make mistakes, and I am not perfect.

Let me give you an example....

I made it my mission this year to work on my health and fitness. My first step towards this was to work on losing weight, so I signed up with a company called "The Fitness Project." I have a health coach (Hi, Jules!), and she helps with a lot of fitness-related things such as meal planning, nutrient counting, and exercise. I also occasionally listen to TFP podcasts and recordings of weekly team meetings hosted by the owners, Brian and Lindsey Pickowicz.

One thing I didn't expect was that this fitness journey would help me regulate my emotions about the food I eat and my weight. I didn't know that I would learn more about my thoughts and their effects on my actions toward my health. In fact, until now, I wasn't even recognizing that I had big emotions about anything related to my weight!

The first day I met with Jules, she told me a number of changes that I would be making to my habits and explained that I needed to weigh myself every day...that these weigh-ins would be simply one piece of data collection to show my progress. This was almost a dealbreaker for me! I really didn't want to weigh myself *every day* (no matter what she was going to call the number on the scale). Throughout the years of trying to lose weight, I hated the scale. Watching it go up and down gave me a pit in my stomach.

Jules somehow convinced me to commit to recording my weight on a daily basis, but I didn't like it. I wasn't able to recognize or label the emotions I had about stepping on the scale every day but looking back on it, I know I felt...

Dread
Regret
Disappointment
Frustration
Fear

Those are the ones I can name at this moment, but I am sure there are more. However, despite all of these emotions, I stepped on the scale and recorded my weight pretty much every day throughout the last year. The good news was that the scale was regularly going down! The exercise and healthy changes to the food I was putting in my body were helping! And I saw results! When the scale went down, my feelings became more pleasant! Along with all of the unpleasant feelings about the act of weighing myself, I felt...

Proud
Accomplished
Successful
Happy
Excited

Those emotions are easier to name for me. The pleasant ones usually are! For most of the last year, I have felt elated at my fitness progress! As a result, I kept up with the hard actions of regularly lifting weights and increasing my muscle tone. I also continued to record my meals every day, watching my calorie, protein, and fiber intake. And I repeatedly watched the scale go down, bringing me lots of pleasant emotions about it all...

Until the end of October.
Last Fall.

That's when I started to notice my weight creeping up. Looking back on it, I was probably getting complacent about all the good habits I created. I went on **one** family weekend out on the boat and didn't eat mindfully. I threw all my good habits out the window. And I came home feeling guilty about it, so I continued my complacent behavior. My old habits and emotions about the number on the scale came creeping back in. And I've been feeling them ever since, but I didn't know it. Once again, I was not recognizing these emotions. I wasn't able to identify how I was feeling, and I didn't know that every time I stepped on the scale, I was feeling more and more...

Discouraged
Regretful
Irritated
Defeated

I was letting my emotions about the scale dictate my thoughts and actions. Sometimes, when I didn't want to weigh myself, I skipped it and chose not to record my weight. I ate things and didn't track them. I overindulged without mindfully asking myself if I was full or if I even wanted to eat what was in front of me.

My emotions about the scale changed my thoughts, which, in turn, changed my actions.

But then everything happened in perfect timing...A weekend

away with family and friends was looming in the distance, weighing on me. So, I reached out to Jules, and she gave me excellent advice. She told me to:

Stay present and have a blast with my family and friends because that is the most important part.
Track (even if it is after the fact).
Put calories at the top of the priority list when making food choices.
Be mindful of my hunger cues.
Pick food I will enjoy and simply adjust portion sizes if I need to.

Whatever happens, it is totally fine.

I felt empowered by her text. And because of this emotion, I had positive thoughts going into the weekend, resulting in me making helpful choices. Was I a perfect angel? Of course not! I enjoyed sweets, cheese plates, cocktails, snacks, and even a Shamrock Shake from McDonalds! I ate very differently than I usually do every day. But it was three days. And I had a mantra in my head, courtesy of Jules...*everything is going to be totally fine*. And it was!

Until the car ride home, when I thought about stepping on the scale the next day.
And that pit in my stomach started to grow.

But suddenly, perfect timing worked in my favor once again! At some point over the weekend, Lindsey, one of the owners of TFP, tagged me in a post about how to manage emotions about weight. Since I was in the car for a four-hour ride home, I had time to plug in and listen to the short video. Everything she said resonated with me. She taught me exactly what I am sharing with you today...that the scale brings up big emotions for me. Those emotions affect my thoughts, which in turn can create actions...some helpful and others not so much! Since emotions are my jam, I ate up everything she said (no pun intended). She asked me to choose something to work on... my thoughts about the scale, my actions, or my emotions.

And, of course, I chose emotions.

To work on my emotions, Lindsey gave me a series of steps to take before stepping on the scale. When I woke up the next morning, I felt ready. I stood in front of the scale, closed my eyes, and took several belly breaths. While I did this, I used the mantra Jules gave me.

Everything is going to be totally fine.
No matter what the scale says.

And I wasn't lying to myself when I said this! Everything was going to be OK. I wasn't going to be hurt. No one was going to laugh at me. My pants would still fit. My pleasant feelings about my weekend away were not going to change.

After a few minutes, I decided how I wanted to feel, no matter whether the scale went up or down. I thought to myself.

No matter what the scale says, I choose to feel proud.

Again, I wasn't lying to myself. I was proud of how I handled myself over the weekend. I was present with my friends and family and fully enjoyed every minute with them. I was mindful of my hunger cues and ate accordingly. I wrote down everything I ate, even if it was after the fact. I stayed hydrated. I was active. I followed all the healthy habits I knew were working for me! So that was it...I chose to feel proud.

And then I did it.

I stepped on the scale.

And the number was slightly lower than it was the morning I left for my weekend away. But it didn't matter because I chose to feel proud of myself no matter what. I went on with my day, and the whole thing was simple, with very little drama. In fact, I can actually say that was the most pleasant experience I have ever had weighing myself! I never thought I'd ever say that!

I know I have a long way to go, and this isn't a one-time-thing. I will continue to weigh myself every day. I will weigh myself tomorrow and the many days after that. This new tool that I learned to manage my emotions about getting on the scale will be tested, especially when the number goes up. But I am feeling...

Empowered
Strong
Equipped
Confident

And I am going to hold onto these emotions while I can. I know feelings come and go, so I will have good days and not-so-good days with this internal emotional battle I can have with myself. But this new tool for emotion regulation has me feeling curious, as a good emotion scientist would! Instead of thinking negatively and making unhelpful choices, I am now able to get curious. I ask myself...

Why do I think the scale is telling me this weight today?
What can I do differently?
Who can I reach out to for support?

This tool feels like a safe choice to me, which is why I am sharing all of this with you. I want to share this tool with you in case you need it. Maybe it isn't the scale that gives you a visceral emotional response. Maybe it is something else. Either way, taking deep breaths, telling yourself a truthful, positive thought, and then deciding how you want to feel before getting curious could be helpful.

Believe it or not, I have looked forward to stepping on the scale over these last few days since I learned this new tool. It's weird! Instead of thinking about how much I don't want to do it, I think about how excited I am to decide how I want to feel about the number the scale reveals. My whole mindset has shifted! What a difference one simple change in my approach to challenges makes, and I am forever grateful that I can add this one to my emotion regulation toolbox.

CHAPTER 31

reading my labels

I AM:

Mindful
Fit
An overachiever
A hot mess
An extrovert

These are just some of the labels that I can sometimes give myself. Are they true? Maybe. Sometimes. Not really. I guess it depends....

I know I'm not the only one. I hear so many acquaintances, friends, and loved ones giving themselves labels, as well. I hear the "hot mess" one a lot. Our society likes that label. Some people even wear it as a badge! But I also hear:

I'm the worst parent.
I'm a C student.

I'm not a people-person.
I'm a rebel.

People like to label each other, too:

She's a drama girl.
He's emo.
They're preppy.
They're a smart kid.
He's too shy.
She's trouble.

Parents, kids, teachers! We all do it! It seems like our world is full of labels! We place labels on things other than people, as well… food, clothing, books, movies, and more! And while sometimes these labels are meant to help us, when we get into the business of labeling ourselves and others, that can be harmful if we're not careful.

When we label humans, we often use adjectives to describe character, behavior, or appearance. This can greatly affect the way we see ourselves, the way we allow ourselves to be treated, and our potential. This influence from our labels can go both ways. They can be helpful for our psyche, but the downfall is that they can be painful, as well. The worst part is that sometimes, we aren't intentionally trying to cause harm to ourselves and others with the labels we choose to use.

I started this story with a few of the labels I give myself. Let's take a look at those for a minute and decide how helpful (or unhelpful) they are for me:

"I am Mindful"

Well, I think this label is pretty true about me. I decided to give myself this label when I started to find value in slowing down, enjoying nature, and turning within myself once in a while. This was an exciting discovery that helped me recharge when I felt socially exhausted. With this label, I have explored so many new things in the last decade or so. I received my yoga teacher training certificate. I learned how to meditate twice a day. I have learned countless breathing and visualization techniques that I use and share with my students. I have also become a Social-Emotional Learning Coach. I think this label is a good example of how, when you choose the right words, labeling can make a positive impact on how we see ourselves and our achievements.

Another example of this is:

"I am fit."

This is a new one for me. A year ago, I never would have said that. And it still feels a little bit unnatural to share that label in print. Here's where it came from:

I used to label my body in a very negative way. I would say:

I can't lose weight.
I am a little chubby in the middle.
I have wobbly bits.

I know that I have not been shy about sharing my fitness journey both through my writing and social media. But in the last year, I have been working hard to lose weight. And when I started the journey, I thought that was all I would do. But I have learned so much more about myself. In particular, I have learned that the way I talk to myself and the labels I use greatly affect my progress.

Am I the most fit person in the world? No...that's not the label I gave myself. And I don't call myself "fit" because I can wear a certain size pair of pants or because the scale reads a certain number. I say I am fit because fit people eat well and exercise. And I do exactly that. And because I am fit, I will keep doing that.

So there. This label is helping me, and I'm not going to change that one! How about:

"I am an overachiever."

I mean...who says what the benchmark is for achievement? What does the "over" refer to? Over what? Is there some sort of standard level of achievement that is generally acceptable? Hmmmm...while that's a good thing that I find achievement important, I feel like when I say that about myself, there is a negative connotation and judgment in there somewhere. Like maybe I work *too* hard. That I'm obsessive or a perfectionist, and maybe society is telling me that is wrong somehow. Even as I type this, I can't really figure out if being an overachiever is a good thing or a bad thing...can you? Maybe I need to re-think that label.

"I am an extrovert."

I know there are real psychological tools that measure this personality trait. However, I've never taken any of those measures. I've just decided to give myself that label.

The terms introvert and extrovert are like two sides of a coin... they are opposing traits in people. You are either one or the other. I understand that these labels are meant to describe our attitudes towards our external and internal world, with one being more dominant than the other, depending on the person. However, the problem is that this label promotes a fixed mindset about who we are and how we relate to others.

It seems that society has led us to believe that being an extrovert is a good thing and being an introvert is not. For example, extroverts are described by their strengths, such as being confident and social. However, introverts are often described by their weaknesses, such as being reserved, sensitive, and off-putting. It is really easy for us to pre-judge introverts as being shy and socially anxious, which isn't always the case!

But guess what?! Extroverts like me can also be prone to feeling socially anxious! Sometimes, I feel like I need to play the part of "mayor" or "life of the party" when it actually emotionally and physically exhausts me. And then I feel inadequate. But I keep going because I have labeled myself as an extrovert. And that's limiting to me. Maybe I need to re-think this label, as well.

"I'm a hot mess."

I really want to stop calling myself this. I wouldn't label my kids this way. I wouldn't label my best friend that way. Our society has taken this term in a very light way. We usually giggle over it...on days when we feel like things just aren't going our way and we can't catch a break. But, according to the Merriam-Webster dictionary, this is a figure of speech that implies that someone or something is in a state of "pitiful disarray." And that is what I am labeling myself as? How is this helping me? It's not...that labeling stops now.

So clearly, I have some work to do when it comes to how I label myself. But now I am questioning if I do this to my children or my friends. Do I look at the people I love and categorize them?

I am realizing that I need to be careful. My words have a lot of impact on how the people I care about think of themselves, what is expected of them, how they are treated, and who they become. My labels may also influence (and place limits on) their potential! This is all especially true for my children.

So what do I do?? How do I change my language? Now that I have awareness, I know it is never too late to reframe what I say. If I did it with my fitness, I think I can do it with anything!

Labels are our limiting beliefs. Labels are unfair, but yet we can still unwillingly do it to ourselves and others. Labels can convey something that is perceived to be absolute, which makes them difficult to navigate away from. Attaching negative labels to ourselves and others can make us feel insecure and may even make it more likely for us to react in emotional and unhelpful ways to the world around us. Labels don't have to define us...it is as simple as that.

Awareness is the first step.
Next comes flexibility in our perception of ourselves and others.
From there, we can stop holding ourselves and others back from living our full potential.

To start, I think I will stick with one simple label. One that sums me up pretty well. And one that has never done me any harm:

I am...
Jenny.

And there are a lot of great places I can go from there!

PART 6

lessons in indulgences

CHAPTER 32

my cat is a life coach

I SWEAR I'M NOT A CRAZY CAT LADY. JUST HEAR ME out....

I'm not used to having a cat as a pet. I grew up with a dog and even adopted my own pup in my junior year of college. When I married my husband, our dogs became automatic siblings. Before we had two kids, we had two crazy dogs together. The similarities between pet-parenting and child-rearing can be insanely similar, but I'll save those stories for another day. When our dogs passed away, I always thought we'd get another one sometime in the future.

But then Ella, our daughter, was born. From the moment she came into this world, she was afraid of dogs. As an infant, we would take her for a walk in her stroller, and if a dog came near, she would scream bloody murder. When Ella got older, I watched her shake and sweat whenever a dog headed her way. The poor thing was scared out of her mind, and I knew there was no way we could bring a dog into our house.

The summer before Ella entered Kindergarten, we decided to get a cat. The kids and I did some research and went to visit a few different kittens before we met our future feline family member. Enter Tiller...an orange tabby cat with the most mellow personality I have ever had in a pet. Ella was smitten from the start, and I am pretty sure feelings were mutual for Tiller. Ella would dress him in her doll clothes, push him around in her toy stroller, and carry him in her backpack. At night, he would jump on her bed and knead her back and head until she fell asleep, a tradition that still holds for the two of them today. Tiller belongs to all of us, but he definitely has a special connection with his sister.

However, since I started working from home, he has become a close buddy of mine. I have a little puff pillow behind my desk that he often snoozes on while I work. He follows me around the house, waiting for a treat. He really loves sitting on my laptop, even while I'm trying to type. Tiller also likes to join my classes with kids, often lying on yoga mats or playing with pom-poms from our crafts.

I never thought I would love a cat as much as I love Tiller. He's the perfect cat for our family, and spending time with him and watching him grow with my family has taught me a few lessons that I'm hoping you can enjoy, too!

Here are three things that I have learned from my kitty "Life Coach":

Kitty Coach Lesson #1:
It is the simple pleasures in life that matter

Tiller doesn't need expensive toys or extravagant gifts, and quite honestly, neither do we! Give him a cardboard box, a pom-pom, his meals, a few snuggles, and he is good to go. It is truly amazing how easy it is to make my cat happy. From laying on the warm keys of my laptop to watching the chipmunks play outside our windows, he is fairly self-occupied.

It often makes me wonder if I am that easy to please. When I watch Tiller flop happily around the living room with an earbud cover that he scored from the counter, I can't help but ponder about the little things that bring me joy. After all, they say that the little things add up to be the big things in life. Tiller has inspired me to spend more time observing nature, enjoying time alone, and snuggling under the soft blanket that we keep in our living room. And I savor these moments because they make me happy. What's better than that?

Kitty Coach Lesson #2:
It is possible to land on your feet even after the biggest falls

I can't even count how many times Tiller has fallen out a window. He has a habit of lying in window sills in the sun, pressed up hard against the screen. Every once in a while, the screen pops out, and Tiller rolls off, plummeting to the ground below. And for some reason, this happens more often from our second-floor windows. It amazes us that he falls from such a height and comes out of it unscathed, often meowing at the door, begging to come back inside so he can find another warm sunspot and possibly do it all over again!

Many times, I am afraid of trying something new or getting too comfortable with something. Maybe this is a fear of failure or a fear of complacency. Because of this fear, I may be inclined to pass up on an opportunity because I am afraid that I won't be good at it or I will be disappointed in some way. I don't even give myself the opportunity to see if it will be worthwhile.

Seeing Tiller fall from such a great height, get up, dust himself off, and come back inside inspires me to give more challenges a try. He clearly doesn't fit on a windowsill, but that doesn't stop him from enjoying it, even if he falls once in a while. Wouldn't it be amazing if I took on the same attitude and did the same thing? I don't think I will be trying out sunspots on a windowsill anytime soon. What I mean is, why can't I try something new, even if it doesn't fit or I feel uncomfortable? Who knows? I may enjoy myself! Or, if I fall, it is possible to land on my feet and try again, just like my cat!

**Kitty Coach Lesson #3:
There is something to be said for unconditional love**

Tiller shows us unconditional love. I think this is something that the human race needs to strive to practice every day! Tiller doesn't care what we look like, what we wear, who we hang out with, what our grades are like, who we choose to vote for, or how much we get paid...he gives us a constant show of support and joy every day, all day! He waits at the door like clockwork for the kids to come home from school. He jumps on the couch for a snuggle and a lap to lay on just about every night while we watch TV. There are days when Tiller wants his own space and to be left alone, but he never forgets a fly-by snuggle, a head butt, or a purr—just to tell us he's there, sharing his love.

Could you imagine if the world worked like that? If the world was a place where no one cared if you weren't the prettiest, most talented, smartest, or richest? And they showed you love no matter what?! The lesson of LOVE is the greatest lesson that humans can learn from, and Tiller does it with ease every day!

One of my idols and journalist, Jane Pauley, says,

"You cannot look at a sleeping cat and feel tense."

This is why I probably started writing this story in the first place. I am sitting on one of my living room chairs, squished to one side, while Tiller snores, smashed between my thigh and the other arm of the chair. As I work, I feel relaxed. When I look at Tiller at this moment and give him a pat on his warm tummy, I can't help but feel gratitude for this little furry creature that continues to teach me so much every day.

It is funny how we can find guidance in places where we least expect it. Take a look around...what kind of life coaching can you find?

CHAPTER 33

little rainbows everywhere

BLOCK ISLAND IS ONE OF MY FAVORITE PLACES ON Earth. My family is lucky that every year, we take the boat and visit the island once or twice. We enjoy anchoring in New Harbor, lounging in the cockpit of our boat, visiting the beaches, and swimming. And, of course, we enjoy going to The Oar for a mudslide while our kids hang over the dock using a string and hot dogs to catch crabs.

My favorite Block Island "alarm clock" is the sound of Aldo's Bakery Boat yelling "Andiamo!" to let boaters know that they are there and ready to sell fresh baked muffins, croissants, donuts, and egg sandwiches for breakfast. There is a big part of me that wants to record the sound of Aldo's Boat to make my real alarm clock for the other days when I am home...just to bring me back to my favorite place, even in the dead of winter!

Every time we leave the dock to head for Block Island, my daughter fairly consistently asks, "Can we go to Coast Guard Beach?" And she will keep asking until we arrive and actually take her there. I'm not sure if Coast Guard Beach is the real name of the spit of sand at the entrance to the harbor. We call it that because, along the beach, there is a Coast Guard station. But other than that, it is a fairly no-frills beach.

There is a lot of fun to be had at my daughter's favorite New Harbor spot, however. We enjoy swimming on the beach because there is a giant drop-off that quickly goes from shallow water to over your head in just a few steps. We also enjoy walking down the beach because you can go past the jetty and onto a larger beach with lots of seals and even an ever-changing fort made from washed-up driftwood.

However, my daughter and I love the beach for a reason that makes it unique. There are small rocks and pebbles in every color of the rainbow along the shore at Coast Guard Beach. I've never seen anything like it! And for the last few years, we have been collecting rocks and turning them into temporary beach art.

My daughter and I have made rainbow rock mandalas, circles, hearts, arches, and more! It is amazing how colorful this beach is, and we truly enjoy looking down on the sand or in the water to collect all of this natural beauty to turn it into something for everyone to enjoy...until the ocean decides to wash our creation back out to sea.

I find walking on any beach and searching for treasures incredibly soothing. To me, it is the ultimate way for me to reduce stress. Whether it is collecting sea glass, beautiful shells, or even rocks...it doesn't matter. I am instantly relaxed.

It is fun for me to do these sea-treasure walks with my daughter. I often notice how different our tastes are in what we see for beauty in our collections. My daughter enjoys finding rocks with speckles and shells with patterns, while I prefer colorful rocks and shells with swirls and spirals. This observation got me thinking...how do we, as humans, determine beauty when we all see it so differently?

Every ocean treasure has its own unique qualities...from patterns to color and shape. But each treasure also has its own individual flaws, as well...from cracks and chips to smudges of color and mishaps. Yet, for someone walking the beach, it is also unique in what we find worthy enough to pick up, keep, and/or turn into temporary artwork.

It's funny because it got me thinking about how the world equates beauty with perfection and unreachable standards. But when I looked at the treasure collection we found on Coast Guard Beach, not one of them was flawless! Yet my daughter and I found beauty, joy, and gratitude in each of the treasures we found!

Imagine a world where we look at ourselves and others like we look at beach collections! What if we embraced and accepted life for what it is...unique qualities, flaws, and all? And even further, what if we took the ordinary (like our colored rocks) and turned it into something for everyone to appreciate?

Walking on the beach and collecting rainbow rocks with my daughter was a very simple exercise that we spent quite a bit of time doing (and continue to do at every visit). This beach is a constant state of wonder for both of us. Why can't I take this simplicity home with me into my everyday world? All it takes is a little bit of mindfulness, but what does that look like?

When we begin to find that our inner perfectionist is taking over, it is important to stop and notice that this is happening. Take a break, find a place to be still, and become present. Just like at the beach, simply focus on what is around you. Sometimes, it helps to pick one thing in your surroundings to focus on and study intensely...just like we would study the rocks and shells along the beach. Notice the unique qualities of whatever you decide to focus on. It really helps if you can take this break in nature.

My favorite thing to do when I notice the beauty in small things around me is to savor it...take a picture so that you can go back to that moment anytime that you need it. And remember how that moment made you feel.

Our world today leaves us with chaos all around us, which can bring us down and make us feel overwhelmed. This can also leave us feeling less appreciative of all the small things that can bring us joy and wonder. Coast Guard Beach's rainbow rocks reminded me that the world still has beauty in it—if we find the time to be present and look closely.

In nature, nothing is perfect. On the beach, rocks can be weird shapes, and shells can be cracked, yet they are still beautiful. And together, they create something unique.

Everything in the world has flaws.

Including us.

Yet, we still hold beauty.

And together, we create something quite special.

So, just like my time collecting sea treasures on Coast Guard Beach, it is a choice in how we find beauty in everything…embracing and accepting life and all its imperfections.

CHAPTER 34

buy the latte

THE SUN IS SHINING, AND I'D LOVE TO GO FOR A WALK, but I just don't have time.

Wouldn't it be nice to have a night out with friends? But I feel guilty not spending tonight as a family....

I'd love a yummy, warm, flavored latte, but I just don't need to spend money on frivolous stuff right now.

Do these thoughts sound familiar? Let me explain....

I love being a mom, but it is a tough job. My entire world revolves around my kids, their schedules, and their needs. Want to go for a walk? I can't...my kids will be home from school soon. Want to go out with friends? I can't...my daughter has dance class, and I need to pick her up after. I work from home, so I'm there as soon as my kids walk in the door from school. I often drive them to and from sporting events, activities, and time with friends. I plan meals, pack lunches, and cook breakfasts. And I have very little time for the many things I used to enjoy before I had a family.

Don't get me wrong. I wouldn't change my role as a mom for the world! It is such an honor to be the mother of my son and daughter. I feel like they are true gifts to me. But sometimes, I like to use motherhood as an excuse that robs me of the little pleasures that can bring me just the right amount of joy I need to keep me going.

Sometimes, as a mom, I can start to suffer from what I call "Martyr Syndrome." Because I don't allow myself to be treated here or there, I begin to get resentful, irritable, cranky, and, at worst, depleted. When these feelings set in, my usual mode is to launch into an inner dialogue that sounds something like this...."I do so much for this family, but it is overlooked. No one cares. Everything is always on me."

This is not, in any shape or form, true.

I have an amazing and supportive husband. My family is grateful for all that I do for them. And I know, without a doubt in my mind, that if I asked them to treat me, they wouldn't hesitate to tell me to go for a walk, send me out with friends, or buy me a latte.

I know my signs...and when I get to the point of martyrdom, it is time for a treat. I don't mean that I go out and spend thousands of dollars on myself. I mean that I find the time to do something that is all about me...something that fills my bucket, and it doesn't need to be a grand gesture.

So, other than walks, nights out with friends, and coffee, what do I enjoy? Sometimes, it is just reading a good book or watching a cheesy TV show. Other times, I visit my local farm stand for some fresh veggies or picked flowers. I may pour myself a warm cup of tea or mix up a fun adult beverage. None of these things are expensive or take a lot of time...they just give me the pause and time with my own thoughts that I so desperately need, especially in my role as a mother.

Making time for small treats has a big influence on my happiness. I cannot afford to neglect myself! Just like any "treat," I don't need one every day, but it is nice to have them in moderation. It is all about balance! And how I show up for myself is reflected in how I show up for others.

With my family, I work hard to balance play and rest. My kids and I enjoy reading together...although now that they are older, this doesn't happen as much as it used to. Every once in a while, I purchase something for my family on their wishlist. Why can't I do these things for myself, too?

I like to make a lot of excuses for *why* I can't treat myself. Does this sound familiar?

I don't have time.
It is too expensive.
I have too much to do.

Yet, I find the time and the finances to do these things for other people...no wonder I feel neglected and burnt out! I am doing that to myself. Besides, I know perfectly well that the four dollars I would have spent on a silly little latte for myself, I will probably spend on something else (that most likely won't be for myself).

Some people will say to treat yourself...after all, you only live once! But as a friend reminded me recently, that's not true. You only die once...you live every day. And while I am living here on this Earth, part of my role is to take care of others. Since I am so good at doing that, I need to make it a little easier to take care of myself, so I am giving myself (and all of you like me out there) permission....

Just do it.
Buy the latte.
You deserve it.

CHAPTER 35

my cheesy tv obsession

I AM ADDICTED.

I can't get enough cheesy television.

And this isn't a new obsession.

In high school, I couldn't get enough of the start of reality television mania when I watched *The Real World*. I still have dreams of staying in one of the houses that they used throughout the twenty-four seasons that the show was filmed!

Back in college, I arranged my class schedule around *Days of Our Lives*. I even took early classes so I could be back to my dorm in time to grab lunch and watch it in the common room before I went off to sailing practice. My friends and I would also arrange nights together with wine and snacks to watch *Beverly Hills 90210* and, eventually, *Melrose Place*. This tradition lasted quite a while!

After college, I was also known to watch countless episodes of reality television, such as *Survivor*, *Queer Eye*, and *Laguna Beach*. Don't even get me started on my obsession with *The Bachelor*. When I moved to California for a short stint, I lived down the street from

Matthew Fox. I was heavily focused on catching a glimpse of one of my favorite actors from *Party of Five*.

I have wasted countless hours watching the cheesiest thing on television throughout my years. I just love it!!

This is my favorite time of year...not just because it is the holiday season, but because...you guessed it...I get to watch Hallmark Christmas Movies! I squeeze those in between watching old episodes of my new favorite reality show, *Below Deck Sailing Yacht*.

Yes...I know. It is a sickness. How can an intelligent woman like myself watch trash like this?

It might be rotting my brain...but I can't be alone. I am hoping that at least some of you reading this story right now are thinking, "I'm so glad it isn't just me." So why do we watch this junk? Why are we so obsessed?

These shows are literally the dessert of television. They are sugary, sweet, and addicting! They give me absolutely zero intellectual stimulation and probably kill a few brain cells along the way.

Scientists have done research on the effects of sugar on the brain. This thought made me curious, so I did a little bit of Googling. I learned that, just like sugar, watching reality and other cheesy television programs releases serotonin and dopamine into the brain. These chemicals help us feel a sense of pleasure, happiness, and well-being. So maybe watching this stuff isn't so bad for me after all!

There are a lot of debates about whether or not watching cheesy television, especially reality TV, is good for our overall well-being. I learned that the impact of this kind of television isn't as bad as we think! Some reality shows may be inspiring. Think about shows like *Nailed It* and *Top Chef*. We are literally watching ordinary people, just like us, work hard and achieve their goals. What is more inspiring than that?

We also may choose to watch shows that bring us to different countries and expose us to different cultures. Shows like *The Amaz-

ing Race give us a glimpse into other places around the world, possibly even inspiring us to get out there and explore the world ourselves!

Other reality shows can be inclusive and expose us to individuals with disabilities and those with diverse backgrounds. Think about the show *America's Got Talent*. One season, a disabled singer named Kobi Lee won the show! There are a few talented people who performed on that show, just like Kobi, who certainly inspired viewers to work hard, never give up, and achieve goals!

After all this research, I asked myself the question again...why do I watch this stuff? Here's my answer summed up in a quote I found through my research, as well....

> "Sometimes, the heaviest thing we carry is not the weight of the world, but the weight of our own thoughts."

There's a lot of heaviness in the world. Watch the news for five minutes, and that will have a greater effect on your well-being than twenty years of cheesy television, that's for sure. I have tough weeks. I read horrifying news. I am all too aware of the sadness happening in this world. So, I watch shows where none of that exists. My cheesy television shows take me to a place where there's love, excitement, adventure, beauty, and joy! For me, watching these shows is about entertainment and relaxation, both of which have a positive effect on my mental state.

So, I don't think I'll quit this addiction quite yet. My research is telling me that this obsession isn't one that will hurt me anytime soon. The only stress I have at the moment over it all is...what will I watch tonight? There are so many choices!! Do you feel me?

CHAPTER 36

things we can learn from my favorite reality tv show

MANY OF MY READERS ALREADY KNOW THAT I CAN'T get enough of shows that take me out of my head and the thoughts that can keep me up at night.

For this story, I would like to focus on my favorite reality television show du jour. It is one that I connect with because of my love of sailing, the ocean, the fresh salt air, and the sunshine.

Have you had a chance to check out any of the *Below Deck* reality show series lately? I don't think I'm the only one! I've had many conversations about this show with people like me, who didn't expect to enjoy it. And it seems like a show that appeals to people of many different ages.

There are so many *Below Deck* shows! There's the original *Below Deck* series. But there are also a few spinoffs, such as *Below Deck Down Under*, *Sailing Yacht*, *Mediterranean*, and *Adventure*. I haven't watched all of these yet, but give me time...I will!

Most of the cast of *Below Deck* seem to fall in their twenties to thirties, so while I don't connect to them at the moment (I am a graying forty-six-year-old), watching these people work and interact brings me back to my youth. As a young twenty-something, I never sailed the world as a stewardess, chef, or deckhand. But, my first job out of college was as the director of a sailing program at a yacht club in Los Angeles, California. I had plenty of time around "yachties," as they call them on the show. However, not many of them looked as good as they do in the *Below Deck* series! Another bonus to regularly binge-watching this show on Hulu.

Anyway....I digress.....

Other than watching beautiful people explore gorgeous places on amazing yachts, this show has me captivated. I can't help thinking about the lessons that lay people like us can learn from watching these hunky characters, episode after episode. So, I've come up with a list you may appreciate:

5 Ways to Live Your Life Like a *Below Deck* Cast Member:

1. Make room in your life for those make you happy (and get rid of the rest):
There are people in our lives who help us out and make us better humans. We get along with them, they make us happy, and we show mutual respect for each other. It is our job to decide who we would like to spend time with and who we would rather not.

A good crew on *Below Deck* works the same way! They work together as a team so they look good in front of the guests, resulting in excellent tips. They get along with each other, make each other laugh, and are respectful of the different jobs that need to get done aboard the super yacht they're working on.

It is the captain's job to keep everyone in order, making sure that the teamwork is seamless. Are one of the crew members getting complacent? Being disrespectful? Breaking a rule? No problem! The captain very matter-of-factly says, "You can pack your things and go."

Crew members are easily replaceable. Usually, within an episode or two, the audience gets to see another good-looking crew member take the place of the ones who just don't work well aboard the ship.

Can you imagine if we all did that? Is an acquaintance being disrespectful? Are they not understanding of your feelings? Do they stress you out more than they make you feel good? They can pack their things and go. You have other people in your life that deserve your time and energy!

2. Be clear about what you want:

I really enjoy how assertive and upfront the captain of a superyacht can be on *Below Deck*. He/she takes the opportunity on the first day before a charter begins to clearly state the expectations of working aboard their ship. Throughout the season, the captain has no problem telling someone if their work isn't up to snuff.

Occasionally, something may not meet the captain's expectations. Perhaps a crew member is not immediately answering when they are called on the radio. What does the captain do? They hunt the crew member down and, in a calm but firm voice, tell them that this is unacceptable. Does the crew member make excuses or resist? If so, the captain will gather everyone together and test all the radios in every corner of the ship to be sure their point is well-taken. Calmly and firmly, they will restate their expectations around responding to radio calls.

Can you imagine if we did this with our teenage kids about responding to our texts? Those of you who have a teenager know that sometimes they don't respond when you want to know where they are, when they'll be home, or when you have to remind them about something. That's the whole reason why we give them these handheld computers in the first place, isn't it? If we were as clear about expectations and rules with our crew at home as the captain is with his crew aboard his ship, there wouldn't be any room for excuses. I am going to work on channeling my inner captain the next time I need to discipline my kiddos. I will be clear and to the point.

Another thing I look forward to while watching *Below Deck* is the episode before each charter, where the captain sits down with the chef, head stewardess, and bosun to review "preference sheets." These are detailed forms that guests complete before a charter to share personal information on preferences related to food, liquor, or any medical needs for the crew to know before they come on board. The preference sheet also gives guests the opportunity to share what they would like to see during their stay aboard the yacht.

Wouldn't it be nice if we all walked around with preference sheets? That might not be feasible, but it is OK to tell someone when you do or don't like something. It is also OK to share your expectations! I think expressing these wants, likes, and needs with others would make life a lot easier and help avoid disappointment and confrontation more often!

3.) Play! Play! Play!

The cast members of *Below Deck* work hard. They cook, clean, and provide entertainment constantly for the guests they are serving. When the guests aren't enjoying a twelve-course themed meal, you can find them playing aboard the ship. The deck crew has tons of toys around, and the guests don't ever seem to be afraid of playing with them! They enjoy giant blow-up water slides, rope swings, floaties, games...you name it! The crew does everything they can to make sure the guests are entertained, and they seem to really enjoy every minute of their time away from reality.

The crew does the same thing when the guests aren't on board! When they're not working, they make the best of their downtime, too! They eat like royalty at gorgeous restaurants, they party hard, they dance, they swim, and they seem to make out with each other quite a bit!

What do you do in your downtime? I can often be found catching up on laundry or planning the next meal...boring and not fun at all! I'd really like to be reading a book or going out to dinner. But I don't often think of the value in making the most of my downtime through play! When was the last time I went down a slide, played a game, ate like royalty, or danced (when it wasn't a wedding)? I could use a little fun like that in my life. And there's nothing wrong with spending downtime with a little kissing (wink, wink)! The crew of *Below Deck* certainly works hard and plays hard. I think I might need to take a page out of that book!

4.) Teach your children well

No...we don't often see the cast of *Below Deck* with their children or families. But we do see the head crew members training their teams like an adult may teach a child. When a new crew assembles, the Bosun and the Head Stewardess spend quite a bit of time guiding their crew through the different daily tasks expected of them. The Head Stewardess shows the Junior Stews how to make a bed, clean the bathroom, serve the guests, squeeze the fresh citrus fruits, work with the chef, and more! The Bosun shows their deckhands how to swab the deck, tie knots, dock the boat, and communicate with the captain while underway. Once this is done, the yacht runs like a well-oiled machine.

Can we do the same thing with our families at home? Absolutely! We can teach our kids how to do the laundry, fold it, and put it away. We can show them how to make simple meals and clean up afterward. We can instruct them how to run a lawn mower and rake the leaves. These things are life skills, and our children will need them more than most skills they learn in school! Not only will our houses run smoothly, but our children will be truly ready to take care of themselves, their homes, and others when they leave the nest!

5.) Love! Love! Love!

This is my favorite thing to learn from the cast members of *Below Deck*! While there is always drama aboard the superyacht, which is fun to watch, there is also a lot of love going around! Crew members fall for each other. We watch them court each other and go on dates. Sometimes, if we are lucky, we watch them get caught in love triangles.

The crew is always willing and ready to support guests who are feeling the love, too! They often help guests who would like to propose to their partner or want to celebrate an anniversary. They also help the guests celebrate by preparing a special party to mark the occasion. One of my favorite episodes featured a group of friends who wanted to celebrate with a Pride Party. The crew went all out with this one, and everyone seemed to have a good time. When their charter was over, as the guests were handing the crew their tips, they expressed how wonderful it was to feel accepted aboard the boat. The crew always seems to understand and celebrate love in all its forms. How great would the world be if everyone did that?

So yes...these are the things I think about when I'm watching my cheesy reality television like *Below Deck*. I'm not just zoning out like a drooling zombie. I am learning from these beautiful cast members and thinking about how I can live a more fun, carefree, and fulfilled life.

So next time you are indulging in something a little cheesy, relishing in the drama, and enjoying the beauty of the offering, ask yourself...what can I learn from this? It'll make the time you're spending on it much more valuable!

PART 7

lessons in holidays and seasons

CHAPTER 37

putting up with winter

THIS WEEK MARKED THE OFFICIAL FIRST DAY OF WINTER. I wish I could get excited about that, but to be honest, the end of a warm summer and vibrant fall season is a downer for me. The days can get tough when the leaves fall off the trees, the holiday season ends, and everything starts to look gray. I find it hard to be motivated, and I just feel blah.

I know I am getting the winter blues because emotions that don't normally come up in the sunny season bubble to the surface. I begin to resent the chores around cleaning my house, like laundry and dishes. The kids and their friends all come inside rather than running around the yard. They can get loud, and it feels annoying. And I get tired easily. I literally finish work, and as soon as the sun sets, I am in my pj's. With the short days, I begin to hibernate, unmotivated to hang with friends or even go out with my husband in the evenings! It's not that I hate my house or my children. It's also not that I don't want to see my friends or spend time with my loved ones. It's just winter. And winter is not my season. Can anyone out there relate to this?

I try hard to become one with winter. I enjoy skiing and snowshoeing...well, kind of. I like being outside and in the mountains. I like seeing the snow on the trees. I like the idea of a warm drink snuggled under a blanket by the fireplace. But I DON'T like being cold, having my eyelashes freeze, or driving on icy roads.

But I really do try. I get excited when snow is in the forecast. I like the look of winter hats and cute snow boots. I honestly look forward to spending all day on a mountain, enjoying the slopes with my family. In fact, time outdoors in the winter makes me feel a lot happier, which is why I do it!

I've lived in climates where there is really only one season, despite what the calendar says...where the weather is always warm and getting outside for some sunshine is pretty easy. You know the crazy thing about me living in these temperate areas? I miss the change of seasons! Even though I get antsy and bummed out in the wintertime, I miss it when I don't have it. I now realize, as I type this, that I am a complex individual when it comes to my feelings about the change of seasons. Haha!

The holidays are almost a thing of the past this year, and I know we are going into what I call the "doldrums" of winter. I have anxiety just thinking about going through the months of January, February, and March...until the hope of spring comes around. I've decided this year that the only way I am going to get through these long, dark, and cold winter months is to remind myself to feel the good I have in my life. So, I made a list to reframe some of my winter doldrum thinking:

When I complain about...

...my house to clean, *I think about the fact that I have a safe place to live.*

...laundry to wash, fold, and put away, *I think about the fact that I can afford nice clothes to wear.*

...dishes to clean, *I think about how I always have food to eat.*

...a noisy house, *I think about how lucky I am to be surrounded by a loving family.*

....how much I hate being cold, *I think about how grateful I am for a warm house, warm clothes, and a loving family to snuggle with.*

...going out in the cold to hang out with my friends and loved ones, *I think about how time with them is such a gift.*

....the cold, dark winter, *I think about how great summer will feel when it finally arrives.*

As Dolly Parton once said,

> "The way I see it, if you want the rainbow,
> you gotta put up with the rain."

I take what she says to mean that I can't take all the good in my life for granted. If I didn't feel the cold of winter, I'd never appreciate the warmth of summer. And I know someday, I'll miss the kids, their friends, and their activities. My house will be quiet, and I'll miss the days when the kids made a racket, produced a mountain of laundry, and created a messy kitchen. As I get older, it will be physically harder and harder to get out in the winter, to walk in the snow, and to hit the slopes. My family, friends, and summer seasons are my rainbows. So, for now, I'll put up with a little rain (or snow) and cold temperatures this winter so I can continue to relish in and be grateful for all I have. Who's with me?

CHAPTER 38

resolutions are a thing of the past

DURING THE WEEK BETWEEN CHRISTMAS AND NEW Year's, I traditionally spend time reflecting on the year that is wrapping up and the changes I'd like to make for the year ahead.

There was a time in my life when I set New Year's Resolutions as part of my reflection. Oftentimes, I forgot about my resolutions well before spring, never meeting them and often feeling like a failure. I have read that I am not alone in this. Research suggests that only nine percent of Americans who make New Year's Resolutions actually complete them. Research also says that twenty-three percent of people quit their resolutions by the end of the first week, and forty-three percent quit by the end of January. These statistics got me thinking…why are resolutions so hard to stick to? Here's what I've concluded….

I think that my resolutions of the past, more or less, were a statement to change something I wanted to fix about myself. Therefore, they inspired negative thoughts about my current situation. Then, after I set them, my resolutions felt like lofty goals that were nearly impossible to reach! As a result, I put more pressure on myself than ever to create change. My resolutions focused on the negative aspects of my life, put a spotlight on what I was lacking, and became too strict. My "all or nothing" mentality about it all gave me very little flexibility, creating a perfect storm to set me up for failure.

Wow...I have never put those thoughts on my New Year's Resolutions down on paper or said that out loud before! When I write it like that, it is no wonder that I no longer have the desire to set New Year's Resolutions.

As an alternative, I like to set what I call "New Year's Intentions." What is the difference between an intention and a resolution? Good question! I wish I knew who said this, but it seems like a fitting way to begin....

> "Time is not refundable. Use it with intention."

The biggest difference between an intention and a resolution is that my intentions approach my goals with more compassion for myself, making me feel less pressured and more inspired. Intentions don't imply that something is wrong with the way I currently live my life. In fact, it simply inspires and motivates me to live even better. My intentions focus on the positive, highlight what I have in my life, and are adaptable, which seems to work for me!

People set intentions all the time! I often set intentions for my day as part of my morning meditations. I've also set intentions for my yoga practice at the start of class. Intentions are something to live by that we can carry with us throughout the day, a moment, or, in this case, throughout the year (and years to come!). When an intention is set, we are choosing to live more mindfully and open to new outcomes. So, how can you go about setting an intention for the new year (or any time of year, really...)?

I learned how to do this from reading a "Thrive Yoga & Wellness" blog post back in 2020. It says, to go about setting a powerful intention in the new year, do the following:

1. Be clear about what you want to cultivate in your life to create an intention.
2. Create an affirmation around your intention (that's an "I am" statement that you can repeat to yourself in the present tense as if it is already true).
3. Simplify your intention into a one-word mantra.
4. Write down your intention, affirmation, and mantra. Save it on your phone, repeat it to yourself during meditation, yoga, breathwork, or anytime throughout your day!

Here are some examples of intentions. If you like them, feel free to use them. But I encourage you to be creative and try writing your own unique ideas! I figured a few examples may help clarify how to make an intention. Here are a few:

INTENTION: I want to work in a job where I feel happy, valued, and challenged.
AFFIRMATION: I am worthy of my dreams, and I am on my way to making them a reality.
MANTRA: Success

-or-

INTENTION: I want to live a healthy lifestyle by losing weight and exercising more often.
AFFIRMATION: I am healthy and capable of taking good care of my body.
MANTRA: Health

-or-

INTENTION: I intend to save money so I can support and contribute to my family and live more comfortably.
AFFIRMATION: I am responsible with my spending, and I'm on the path toward increasing my savings.
MANTRA: Abundance

The key to these intentions is writing your affirmations and/or mantra down and putting it in a place where you can see it throughout the day. This serves as a reminder to keep yourself focused on your intentions. If your intention is to live a healthy lifestyle, but you notice that you have not been walking about your days in line with your intention, repeating the mantra can help steer you back to where you want to be. These intentions, affirmations, and mantras are gentle and loving nudges to keep you on track for cultivating your desires in life!

Writing this has made me excited to form my own intentions for the new year. I clearly haven't done that yet...these things take time. They are "intentional" after all, which, according to my Webster's dictionary, means created "by design." We have the power to design, create, and manifest anything we'd like with the time we have left on this planet...why not take some time to do it with purpose?

CHAPTER 39

a gift from the heart

MY FIRST TEACHING JOB WAS IN THE INNER CITY OF Los Angeles, California. I was twenty-one years old and extremely naive. I had never really left my home state of Rhode Island for long and lived a more sheltered life than I realized. I had no idea the level of poverty and inequality that existed around our country until I started working as an educator.

I was very excited to start this new job! I spent a lot of money and a good amount of my days leading up to the start of the school year decorating my classroom. I bought a cute rug and some bulletin board embellishments. I bought fun supplies and set up elaborate learning centers. I couldn't wait to meet my new students! I had no idea that they would teach me more than I was going to teach them that year....

Have you ever seen the movie *Training Day*? Part of that movie was filmed in the neighborhood where I was working. It was a highly transient neighborhood, meaning that many families would live there until their lease ran out or they were evicted and then moved a few blocks over, where their children would attend another school.

I taught in a multi-age classroom of fourth and fifth graders. There were thirty-two students in my classroom. However, I calculated that I actually taught close to seventy-five students that year, with kids moving in and out and sometimes back to the neighborhood.

The student population was fairly diverse. However, there were very few students who weren't of African American or Asian descent. I was one of two teachers that were not of color. I quickly learned that I was not a well-loved addition to the school faculty. It took a long while before the adults and children in the building warmed up to me.

On my first day of school, I stood at my desk and greeted students as they entered my classroom. I warmly said hello, handed them a little packet of school supplies, and directed them to find their labeled seats. One of the first students to walk into my classroom stopped, looked me up and down, and exclaimed, "Aw man! I don't want no white teacher!" I could immediately see that I had some work to do to show these kids that I really wanted to get to know them, be their teacher, and give them as much love as I could despite our cultural divide.

It took a while to earn my students' respect. I had to show them that even though our backgrounds and race differed, I was their ally. Slowly, we began to get to know each other, and I think I was somewhat accepted by them and eventually my colleagues.

It was at this school that I received one of the best gifts I have ever been given. It was the day before the winter holidays, a typical time when students bring their teachers' presents. Throughout my twenty years, I have received countless boxes of candy, candles, mugs, ornaments, and more. This year wasn't any different! My students made me cards and wrote notes that I still have to this day. I honestly never take anything my students and their families give me for granted.

One of my students walked into my classroom a little bit late for the start of the day. She told me that she had something for me but wanted to give it to me before recess. I smiled and told her I couldn't wait.

When the time came, the other kids left my classroom for the playground, and she approached my desk. From her coat pocket, she pulled out a bright blue and melted freeze pop. Before she handed it to me, she said that she was sorry it had melted. When I looked up at her, her eyes sparkled as she told me that her mom only gets these pops on special occasions, and blue was her favorite flavor. It was the last one in the box when she pulled it from the freezer for me that morning.

My eyes welled up at the thoughtfulness of this gesture from my student. Here, this child stood before me with a gift in her hand that she could have kept for herself. I could tell that this gift was very special for her to give to me, and I felt honored.

On almost every special occasion, we carefully choose and offer gifts to our loved ones. It is something we do naturally, and most of us don't think about its deeper implications. Yet, the gift we choose and how we present it says so much about us and our relationships.

This blue and melted freeze-pop gift was a true expression of love and appreciation from my student to me. With no words, this small gesture told me that she cared about me and enjoyed being in my classroom. Our relationship was so bonded that she saw the blue pop in her freezer that morning and felt called to share it with me. My student acknowledged me in the most unique and meaningful way, and I felt so grateful in that moment.

There are times that I wonder if we've lost our way a little bit when it comes to the meaning of a gift. Our culture is so focused on consumption. A gift, by definition, is something given willingly to someone without payment. It isn't about frantically shopping sales or responding to every ad-induced impulse that comes our way. It isn't about spending a lot of money. It is about checking in with ourselves, our friends, and our family and finding a way to spark joy in each other's lives. It is about being thoughtful.

And wow...this student was so incredibly thoughtful in her gift to me that day.

I asked her to walk with me to the teacher's room so I could put it in the freezer to enjoy later. We chatted the entire walk together, and I could see her happiness as I carefully placed it in a spot where no one else would take it.

The next day, after lunch, I opened my blue freeze pop while my students were silently reading. I made a big display out of cutting it open and tasting it. I could see the joy in my student's eyes as I ate her popsicle. I wrote her a note that afternoon thanking her for my gift and telling her that I am now a new lover of blue-flavored freeze pops.

I think of this student every Christmas when I receive gifts from students, and every summer when I eat freeze pops with my kids. I always eat the blue ones first. I wasn't lying when I said I was a new blue pop fan. Twenty-five years later, I still appreciate and love the best gift I have ever been given...a gift that held a lot more meaning than just "thank you for being my teacher."

This gift from my student truly meant more to me than just the physical object she handed me that day. It became a symbol and reminder of the unique bond teachers can share with their students. The special things that kids give the adults in their lives speak volumes about your relationship with them. That "thing" can be a freeze pop or...

A dandelion from the backyard.
A pencil drawing.
A handmade card.
A craft from school.
A handmade piece of jewelry.

Whatever the item may be, it is a symbol of a child's admiration and respect for you. It is love in its purest form...something it is important to spread around these days!

My student taught me that not every gift we give has to be life-changing. And that a meaningful gift doesn't have to cost a lot of money. Gifts are about expressing love...it is as simple as that! This student didn't live in a world where material possessions were abundant, yet she chose the most intentional and considerate gift I have ever been given. She taught me something that day that I will never forget.

CHAPTER 40

emerging from my hibernation

IT IS AROUND THIS TIME OF YEAR THAT I FEEL LIKE A bear coming out of hibernation. I mean...humans can't **actually** hibernate, but in the coldest months of the year, I am drawn toward something like it. After the holidays and into January until the first signs of spring, I want to batten down the hatches from the harsh weather outside and preserve my energy. I want to skip going out for my errands and begin to drag my heels on taking the outdoor walks that I know are good for me. And social interactions feel like an imposition. I do everything I can to resist the urge to pull my comforter over my head and hide.

Is it such a bad thing to desire hibernation until spring?

At the very least, it does feel like a natural response to slow down in these colder months. While I enjoy the solitude and reflection that the winter season can bring, I can't wait for the sun to shine longer throughout the day, for the grass to turn green, for the birds to sing loudly, and to soak up the warm, fresh air!

However, last Sunday afternoon brought me out of my winter slumber. I woke up in the morning to the sound of several birds chirping in my yard and was pleasantly surprised to see a blue sky and sunshine. The thermometer outside my house read close to fifty-five degrees, which is practically a heat wave in New England this time of year! I couldn't wait to get out for a walk! This was a nice change to the reframing and pleading I've had to do in my head just to get myself outside for a walk all winter long.

Last Sunday morning, I couldn't lace my sneakers fast enough!

I turned on my Spotify playlist and put it on shuffle. Ironically, the song *Sunshine* by Caroline Jones was the first song that began to play as I took my first steps. She sang...

There may be gray skies
But when it rains, I can feel the sunshine
I feel the sunshine
And that which I feel
I know to be real
The vision I hold when winter's so cold
I can feel the sunshine

It was fate that this song began to play because, finally, the gray skies were clearing, and I was ready to soak up some sun! If there weren't people around me and I wasn't risking embarrassing myself, I would have danced on the sidewalk because being out in the almost-spring weather felt so incredibly pleasant! I saw crocus and tulips poking out of lawns that I passed. There were kids with their families on our local beach playing with pails and shovels. Friends gathered on benches to sit, chat, and enjoy a coffee together outside. The townspeople were emerging! It felt like I wasn't the only one coming out of hibernation at that moment! And my entire mood...my entire being...changed with that small dose of Vitamin D I gave myself that afternoon.

If it wasn't for the winter season, I don't think I would appreciate the sunshine and warm weather as much. I lived in Southern California for a brief time back in my twenties, so I know that feeling the change of seasons and "wintering" isn't a universal human experience. While living in the land of sunshine and beaches for that brief period of time, I definitely took the warm weather for granted. But as a true New Englander, I recognize that the seasons are nature's way of reminding me that I have to go through the dark, cold days in order to truly enjoy and relish all that spring and summer can bring to me.

This is a great metaphor for my emotions, as well! I often teach my students that emotions and feelings are like waves on the ocean....

When we find a pleasant wave, we enjoy and "surf" it!

When we find an unpleasant wave, we brace ourselves and duck-dive under it.

When a wave knocks us down, it is OK to get back up and try again.

Just like waves on the ocean, our feelings will come and go. They are not permanent. It is how we move with them that matters.

But after Sunday's walk, I am seeing that it is important to see emotions like the seasons, as well....

We will have dark days and bright days, but no matter what, the days will pass.

Just like there are dark emotions, there are bright emotions that aren't permanent, either.

In the winter, we have tools to keep us warm: blankets, jackets, hats, mittens, and fireplaces. In the summer, we have tools to keep us cool: sprinklers, lemonade, ice cubes, and air conditioning.

We can use these tools to help us feel more pleasant until these days pass. But none of these tools actually change the seasonal weather.

Just like the tools we have to regulate our emotions! The tools don't take the emotions away; they just make life more tolerable until we move through those feelings.

Depending on the season, we notice the sensations in our bodies (goosebumps, sweat, shivers) to decide which tool to use to make us more comfortable.

Our emotions also change sensations in our bodies (heart beats faster, tense muscles, breathing changes). Noticing them will help us label the emotion and decide which tools we need to move through the feeling.

Sometimes, we forget our tools (like our jackets or the right shoes), but we still manage to get through the unpleasant sensations this may bring us. And next time, we won't forget!

Just like we make mistakes and forget to use our tools, resulting in an inappropriate reaction to an emotion, but that is OK...there are ways to move on and learn from those mistakes.

There is no **bad** or **good** season...they are simply seasons that sometimes feel pleasant or unpleasant to us. And everyone has their own preference as to what climate they'd like to spend more time in!

Just like there are no good or bad emotions, it isn't bad to be angry or good to be happy. It is simply pleasant or unpleasant, and we have choices on how we want to respond to these emotions.

There is a purpose behind each change of season! If we didn't have the change of seasons, there wouldn't be new life.

There is a purpose behind the change in our emotions, as well! If we didn't have different emotions, we wouldn't learn and grow!

Maybe your favorite season is winter, with fresh powder snow and cold mountain air for skiing. Or maybe it is the summertime with warm sunshine on your skin and refreshing water for swimming. It could also be something in between! No matter what, the next time you relish it, remind yourself that you would never truly enjoy that feeling if you didn't feel the opposite.

Although winter isn't my favorite season, I have learned to live with it and relish the rest and relaxation that it can bring me if I let it. Even though I want to jump on the first plane to warmer weather, I have learned not to avoid the colder temperatures. I've learned to find things on those cold days that make it more tolerable.

It is important to do the same thing with the unpleasant emotions that all humans feel from time to time. Winter may make me feel like I want to go into hibernation, pulling my comforter over my head and shutting out the world. But I try really hard not to do that. Avoiding my unpleasant emotions won't make them go away…just like hibernating won't stop the cold weather from coming. I know that feeling all the feelings is an important part of the human experience. As author Dave Matthes says,

> "Embrace all emotions: sadness, happiness, sorrow, hate, love, prejudice, fear; they are all weapons against our greatest enemy: indifference."

So while hibernating and finding time to slow down in the colder months isn't a *bad* thing, I have to be careful that I don't miss out on some winter fun…and there is some if I look for it. Otherwise, I risk becoming detached from all the abundance that the seasons (and my emotions) can bring me.

CHAPTER 41

slowing down, not speeding up

THE OTHER DAY, I WENT TO THE PHARMACY TO PICK UP some medicine for my son. The woman behind the counter looked very harried. She was moving around her space at a high rate of speed. Her eyes were wide open as if she was really feeling the pressure. She asked me to wait a few moments while she finished something. Feeling her stress, I told her not to worry...that I would sit down until she was ready and take as much time as she needed.

When she was done, she called me back to the counter, thanked me for giving her time, and apologized that I had to wait. I told her there was no need to say sorry! She was busy, and I understood. Then we did what friendly strangers do...we talked about the weather.

It has been really humid here lately, but this day felt like things were finally drying out a bit. It was a truly gorgeous afternoon! A perfect ten of a day! While we were discussing this, I told her that I planned to just stop everything I was doing later that afternoon so I could get out and enjoy it. Her response was, "I wish the whole world would just stop for one day so I could enjoy it, too!"

I made a joke about how everything shuts down around here

when we get snow...why can't we get a day off when it is so beautiful out, too? Wouldn't it be nice if the whole world could stop like that?

We both agreed yes...if we ruled the world, we would slow everyone down rather than speed them up! Because here's the thing...we live in a really fast-paced world. It seems that most of us equate success with how fast and how much we are able to accomplish. But at what cost? If that woman continued working at that pace every day, all week long, she was going to burn out!

It seems to me that the happiest people I know are those with the knowledge that slowing down is where you find happiness. Happiness isn't the hamster wheel of perpetual proving, busyness, and worth-seeking that our society tends to find itself. Speed and pressure just aren't sustainable for any human being on this earth!

When I say "slow down," I don't necessarily mean stop. The imaginary world of our governor calling a day off and requesting we all stay home because the weather is just too gorgeous out isn't realistic.

But...let's go back to the pandemic for a second...that was a time when the whole world truly did completely shut down. Everything stopped. And that was stressful. But there was a weird little part of me that was happy to not have to run my kids around to a thousand different places in several different directions. Suddenly we were eating more dinners together as a family and watching movies together. We had more *time* to just be. And that was wonderful! I remember saying out loud to my husband, "When this is over, I think I want to keep the slower pace that we find ourselves in right now."

>But here we are.
>Back at full speed.
>Riding the hampster wheel.
>And wishing we could slow down!

But do we have to wish? Why can't we just do it? Why is choosing to slow down, enjoy time together with the people we love, and reduce our stress so impossible? *Because we live in a time when feeling stressed and being busy is expected and respected.*

But we can change that.

I know that sometimes it doesn't feel that way, but we have choices about how we spend our time. Maybe we don't sign our kids up for *every* activity they want to do. Maybe we can prioritize our task list so that we do what we can manage in the time that we have. Perhaps we ask for help so that we don't have to do it all by ourselves. Perhaps we should start using the word "no" a little more often to create boundaries between what we want to do and what is asked of us.

This visit to my local pharmacy got me thinking...how can I create my own snow day? How can I create time where I slow down, take care of myself, and be with my friends and family?

So I took out my calendar and started to make space...space for the things that fill me up...space for the people I love...and space for *me*.

Watching the woman behind the counter at the pharmacy, I could see how depleted she was feeling. Her cup was empty, and she was exhausted. I thought about the people at home who would be counting on her when she returned from work...would she have anything left to give them? Probably not....

How we show up for ourselves is a direct reflection of how we show up for others. If we don't slow down and take care of our basic needs, how can we do that for others? The answer is simple. We can't.

The more that I think about it, the more I realize that we have no choice but to slow down. Something *has* to give, or we aren't going to make it.

So, where do we start? I am beginning by thinking about what my time means to me. Me-time is valuable...without it, I can't recharge. And time with my loved ones is valuable...catching up, listening to their stories, and having experiences builds my connection to them.

Work time? I can't say it isn't valuable...it is how I support my family. But I will say that there is **no job** that is worth my health and the health of my relationships.

And the time I spend hustling and bustling? That just seems like wasted energy. I can definitely prioritize my time so that I'm not always rushing my life away.

So, my time is worth something to me. And it is worth a lot. That focus will center on me next time I find myself running around like a chicken with my head cut off. I need to be in tune with my body when I am in stress-mode. When I feel my heart racing, my muscles tensing, and my eyes popping, then I know it is time to put a hard stop to whatever I am doing...take a few breaths...and re-evaluate what I am doing with my valuable time.

Slowing down means I can enjoy the moment.
Slowing down means I can be more productive.
Slowing down means I can better show up for myself and others.

Can I say the same about speeding up? Not a chance....

CHAPTER 42

perpetual sundays

AUGUST.

Every educator's least favorite month.

It is the month that continually reminds teachers that both summer and freedom are over. It is no coincidence that August and anxiety both start with "A." The first day of August feels like the beginning of perpetual Sundays....the time when we feel like we haven't done enough, we aren't prepared, we haven't enjoyed summer to its fullest, and now it is almost over.

When I taught in a public school classroom, I became a different person come August. I used to joke with my other educator friends that my husband likes "July Jenny" way better than "August Jenny." The second that July was over, I started to think about everything I needed to do before the school year started and everything I didn't do that I wanted to do over the summer.

Many August mornings, I would wake up with a weight on my chest. I had trouble falling asleep on many August nights. August just plain stunk, and it affected my entire family. There is a special place in Heaven for partners of educators...the patience and understanding that they have to set forth come August is truly extraordinary. I see my current educator friends feeling the same way now that the calendar has turned to the last month of summer, and I feel for them.

Only people working in the field of education really understand the feeling of August anxiety. Many of my friends and family members outside of the classroom often scoffed when I told them how stressed I felt about summer ending. They'd say, "At least you have the summer months off." I know when I'd complain that I sounded spoiled, so eventually, I stopped talking about how I was feeling. So, it came out in other ways...

I cried easily.
I didn't sleep.
I absorbed myself in "to-do" lists.
I became irritable.

And the worst part of it all was that in August, I stopped enjoying summer. I tried really hard to tell myself to soak up every last minute. I would schedule fun summer activities with my family, but they felt like they were crammed, and if they didn't go perfectly, they were ruined.

Some of my friends describe their August anxiety as crippling. I know it isn't that they don't *want* to go back to school. In fact, I can speak for myself when I say it is the exact opposite. I always felt excited about meeting new students. I loved setting up a new classroom! I loved shopping for new classroom supplies. The thought of a new school year wasn't the issue.

I am going to say this out loud, and it might sound crazy...but here goes. *Teaching is all-consuming.* Yes. You heard me. Good teachers live and breathe their jobs. They don't close their computers and put them away at the end of the day before they go home. They carry their students, their lessons, and their whole classroom everywhere they go. Why? Because they care...more than anyone understands.

Educators are the most committed people I have ever met! They come into work early almost every day, well before contracted time, to set up their classroom for the day, make copies, lay out supplies, and answer emails. They spend every free moment that they have while they're in school creating the best lessons and responding to all their students' needs whenever they can! They stay after school to meet with parents or colleagues, plan more lessons, and prepare for the next day. Then, they go home at night to answer more emails and correct papers. They sometimes have a hard time falling asleep because they worry about a student or a colleague.

The job of teaching never ends. It is rewarding but, at the same time, exhausting. It takes a village to raise children...and teachers are part of everyone's village in the neighborhood. They spend more time with children than most of their families get in a work week. They know perfectly well how important their role in a child's life is. This is a lot of pressure for one human being!

The statistics are staggering. According to the Pew Research Center, seventy-seven percent of teachers say their job is stressful. Sixty-eight percent say it is overwhelming. Many teachers report that students are not motivated to learn...that students are distracted by their cell phones and other electronics. They also report that students (and sometimes parents) are often disrespectful. A majority of teachers report that they have been verbally abused by their students and/or parents. And many also report that the current discipline practices at their school are very or somewhat mild. With all of this, plus student poverty, chronic absenteeism, student anxiety, and depression, on top of the pressure to perform, it is no wonder that teachers feel this way. This is just too much!

And unfortunately, this pressure can be at the expense of teachers and their families. It affects everyone's health and wellbeing. Teachers give so much to more than twenty-five humans a day, and when they go home, they have very little to give themselves or their families.

This is why August hits educators like a ton of bricks. August means that in a few short weeks, the pressure will be back on. The job will consume them and their families again.

This pressure makes it hard to breathe. It makes it hard to sleep. And all the symptoms of anxiety completely kick in.

I used to try to tell those who don't work in the field of education that every new school year is like starting a new job...there are unknowns, the expectations will be different, and new players will enter the game. The analogy of a new job every year is mild, I know. But it is the only way I know how to explain it.

So what I'm trying to say to all my educator friends is...I feel you. I get it. And your feelings are justified.

August is hard.

But here is my question...is this how you want to show up for your students? Is this how you want to show up for your family? And more importantly, is this how you want to show up for yourself?

I am guessing the answer is no, hence the anxious feelings.

It is time to change the August narrative. August doesn't have to be the end of the feelings of less pressure and freedom from the summer. We are in charge of how we feel, and a calendar flip shouldn't be given that kind of power.

First, it is important to acknowledge the feelings of going back to school...stress, worry, anxiety, and whatever else is swirling around. Write it down and say it out loud. You have to name it to tame it.

Next, write down every worry in your mind about the upcoming school year. I used to worry that I'd have a tough student. I'd worry that I wouldn't have time to do the things I enjoy. I'd worry that something was going to go terribly wrong. Whatever it is, note it and then go through the list. Are there some worries that are far-fetched? Cross them off. Are there some worries that you can run through the worst and best-case scenarios? Tweak them if possible.

Then, make a list of all the things you do in the summer that you want to keep doing throughout the school year. For example, in the summertime, I like that I have time to exercise more. I like that I get a pedicure every few weeks. I like that I have more date nights with my husband. Pick a few non-negotiables on the list that are possible to continue doing throughout the school year and make a promise to stick to them.

Finally, use these non-negotiable things as a way to set boundaries. Maybe this upcoming school year, you go into school early but then leave at the end of the day. Maybe you set a time limit on how late you'll grade papers in the evening. Perhaps you'll make a promise to yourself NOT to check emails outside of school hours. Whatever it is, set boundaries, write them down, and stick to them.

It is possible to hold onto a few feelings from the summer despite the fact that a new, all-consuming school year is coming soon. But we don't have to let a new school year consume us!

Remember, we are in charge...not the calendar!

Teachers work hard. They deserve their summers. They deserve the time in July *and August* to spend with their families and on themselves. Teachers...it is time to take the second half of your summer BACK!

CHAPTER 43

summer's funeral

I HAVE MIXED FEELINGS ABOUT THE KIDS GOING BACK to school.

On the one hand...

I absolutely love the summertime! Besides the weather, I enjoy the longer days, the time spent outside, and the quality time with my kids. Honestly, I love any time spent out on or near the water! I particularly enjoy going for a walk or a run early in the morning without having to wear my headlamp because the sun is already above the horizon.

The other night, my husband and I decided to take a quick dip in the pool under the stars. The water was refreshing, and the sky was crystal clear. It was a gorgeous night with the crickets and the frogs singing to us in the background. As we were toweling off, I said something along the lines of, "I'm going to miss our night swims and our fire pits..." and then I continued to list everything I'll miss about summer.

Like I was reading a eulogy.

And my husband called me on it. He said, "Don't talk like you're at a summer funeral! We still have plenty of summer left."

And he's right. Summer isn't over until the end of September. We often associate the beginning of Fall with the start of school, but that's not true at all! There are still plenty of longish, warm, and sunny days left to enjoy! It's just that the hustle and bustle of the school schedule can sometimes get in the way....

But on the other hand...

I am getting a little sick of the summer shuffle to my kids' various activities and camps. Every week in the summer is different—depending on where my kids signed up to be and when—leaving me to scramble and balance work in between it all. Honestly, parenting and working are a balancing act anyway, but there is something about the irregular schedule that can be exhausting in the summer.

Take today, for example...I woke up to drive my son to his sailing practice about an hour away, two hours round-trip. When I got home, I had just enough time to check my email before my daughter needed to be at her camp. I drove a much shorter distance, but it was still about forty minutes away from my desk. I sat down to work for about a half hour, and then I was out the door for a meeting. By the time I returned home, I only had about twenty minutes before I started working with students. When that was done a few hours later, I had to drive to get my daughter and son all over again. When I returned home, it was time to feed everyone dinner! I didn't even touch my to-do list all day, which is why I am continuing to work in the evening as my household settles down for the evening.

It's a lot.

I'm ready for the back-to-school routine to kick in...where most days have a fairly predictable schedule, and I will maintain pretty much the same routine through the winter.

But...on the other hand...

Wait...how many hands do I have?
Seriously, I told you I had mixed emotions.
I'm sad the summer season is going to end.
I'm happy and relieved to be back in the regular routine of school again.

But I'm also overwhelmed by the back-to-school demands! I've already received quite a few emails from school with forms to fill out, information to know, important dates to mark on the calendar, and activities in which I am required to participate! I can't keep track of it all, and if I don't write it down, it will be forgotten! I have an incredible amount of sticky notes with things I need to remember all over my house....

The change of seasons is just tough! I feel like as soon as I get into a routine, it all changes for me.

But...on the other hand (last one, I promise!)...

How grateful am I that I get to experience it all?
I get to be present with my kids all summer long, enjoying time with them, hearing their stories about camps and their friends, and taking them on warm-weather adventures! I get to see them grow and change as they learn in school. I get to cheer them on at sports games, tell them I'm proud of their accomplishments, and see them thrive with their friends! My kids make me feel so incredibly proud. I am one lucky mom!

Can you see what I'm trying to do here? I'm following the advice from American author and poet Celia Thaxter, who said,

"There shall be eternal summer in the grateful heart."

So, while my thoughts about summer ending can feel funeral-esque, I am aware that summer will return, and I know that I have enjoyed every minute of it this year. The best I can do is feel all the feels, embrace them, and express my gratitude for the time I've been given.

With that, I will carry the "life is good" summer attitude with me for eternity....which sounds pretty good to me!

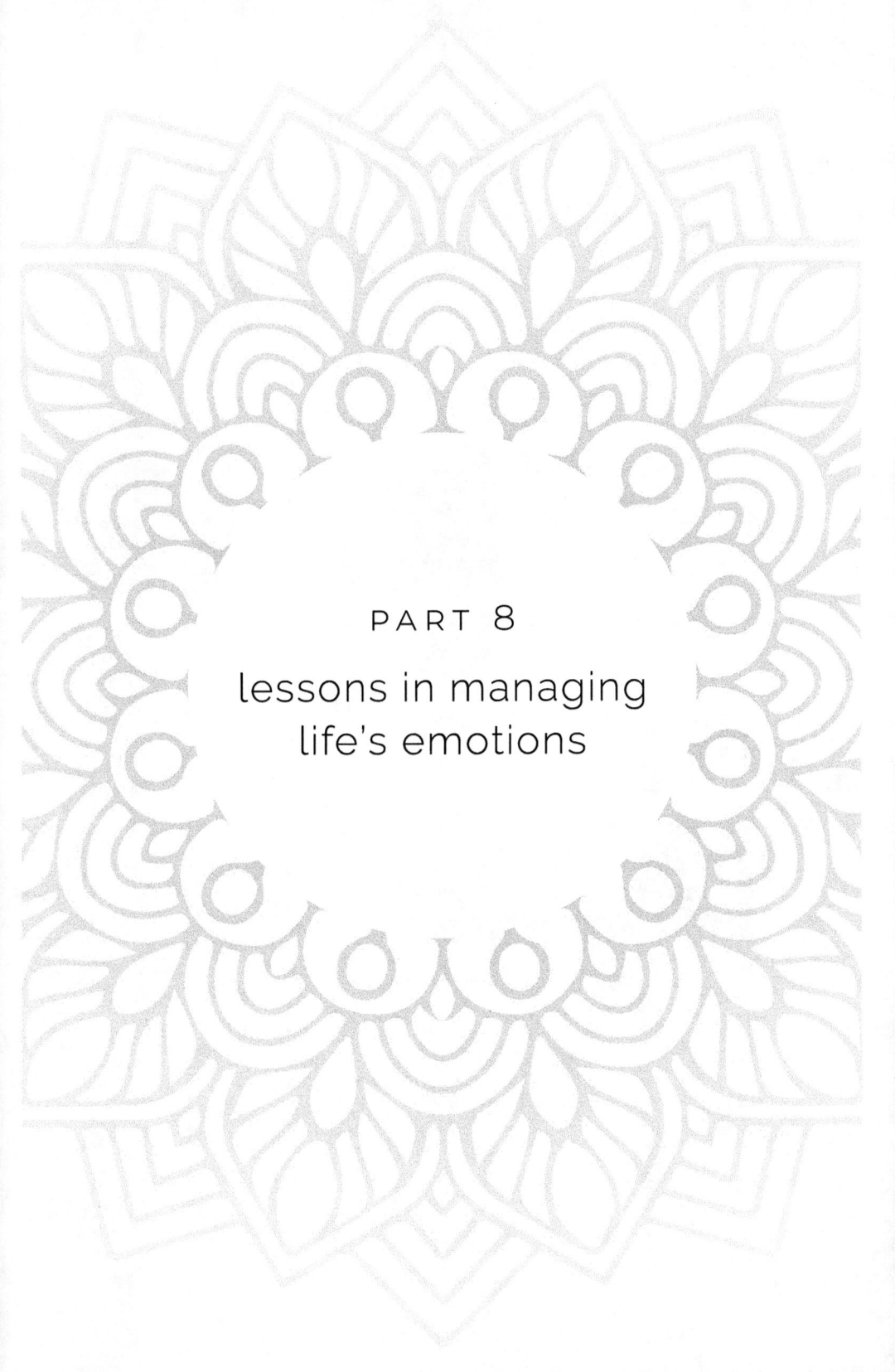

PART 8

lessons in managing life's emotions

CHAPTER 44

the hard emotions

I LOVE TALKING ABOUT EMOTIONS! WHEN I ASK SOMEone how they are feeling, I **really** mean it...I want to know exactly how someone is feeling and why. I am fairly good at naming my emotions, as well. This is something I have learned...none of us were born emotionally intelligent. These are skills that need to be taught, much like math and reading!

Last week, one of my students nearly stopped me in my tracks when they asked me if I have any emotions that I struggle with. I told them, "Of course I do! No one likes the unpleasant emotions...and I struggle with those like every human on this planet."

After she left our session, I reflected a lot on the question that she asked me and the answer that I gave her in return. I began to ask myself...do I really struggle with unpleasant emotions? And the answer I found within myself was a resounding YES! I **hate** unpleasant emotions so much so that I can often be found avoiding them.

I had a friend a while back tell me that they often got annoyed with me for seeing the positive side of things all the time. She was a fellow educator, and on the toughest days...the ones where a student might have such a fit that they clear the classroom. Or the days when it felt like a full moon. Or the afternoons when we would have a really stressful staff meeting…those were the days when I would be a cheerleader for everyone else. I'd try to say positive things in what I **thought** was an attempt to uplift everyone's spirits. But what I am realizing is that it was **actually** an attempt to avoid the anger, frustration, sadness, and disappointment I was feeling at work. And this friend of mine saw right through my positivity.

I don't enjoy feeling unpleasant feelings. And I don't like seeing anyone else have unpleasant feelings, either. Sometimes, I use positive thinking to avoid what I am really feeling. I also encourage others to see the positive side of things as a way of "fixing" how they may be feeling. And I have discovered that this is a really annoying trait!

I noticed this the other day when my daughter was having a meltdown about something that happened at school. In my attempt to "fix" her feelings about what happened, I told her that she needed to see the bright side of things. Immediately, I offered ideas and suggestions on how she could approach the situation in a different way. Her response was, "MOM! You just don't understand!"

I think what she was trying to tell me was that I didn't empathize with how she was feeling, I wasn't validating how she felt about everything, and she wasn't feeling supported. My response was actually adding to her frustration about the situation.

For some of us, showing empathy, giving validation, and offering support is a simple task. And for others, this is something that takes a lot of work. I didn't realize how much work I really needed in this area. I quickly discovered that I needed to manage my struggles with difficult emotions in order to help my daughter manage her unpleasant feelings.

Nine times out of ten, if you ask me how I am feeling, I will tell you that I feel something pleasant, even if I'm not. I don't want to share the unpleasant feelings with anyone because then I have to address the issue that I am feeling unpleasant about.

For example, it is no secret that I have been working on my health and fitness. I set a goal for my weight loss, and I am only five pounds away from reaching that goal. I have been working to lose those last five pounds for almost a year. I have gone up and down the same two to three pounds, and I feel extremely frustrated about it all. Did you hear that? I said *I feel frustrated!* That is really HUGE, and I can share that with you here in black and white. By admitting that I feel frustrated, I now need to dig deeper into what is happening to me here…

I feel frustrated because the scale isn't budging. But I also feel frustrated with myself. I feel like I have a goal, and I suck at reaching it. In my frustration, I am more apt to eat something unhealthy or skip a workout. And when I do that, I feel disappointed in myself. Hear that?? Another unpleasant feeling… ***disappointment.***

When I get disappointed in myself, the negative self-talk sets in:

I'll never be able to do this.
My body is just not meant to be this size/weight.
Why do I even bother spending the time/money?
I am such a failure.

And these thoughts lead me to feel *angry* with myself…the worst unpleasant feeling of them all. I hate being angry.

Positive people aren't angry.

But I am…I am frustrated, disappointed, and angry. And that doesn't sit right with me. So what do I do sometimes? I ignore those feelings with thoughts that don't always sit right with me, but I feel like I need to have them so that the bad thoughts can go away.…

Keep trying…you'll get there eventually.
You look perfect the way you are.
You've come so far!
You can do this!

While these thoughts are good to have, say, and keep in my brain, they don't address the issue that I am having with avoiding my negative feelings. I am not giving myself a chance to express how I am feeling. And in turn, I am not showing up for myself in an empathetic way by validating how I am feeling.

What I need to tell myself is:

You are frustrated, disappointed, and angry. And rightfully so! You've worked so hard, and it is challenging to see your progress on the scale.
There...that's empathy and validation right there.
But I also need to give myself support. So what can I do? What do I need? I need to work on my self-talk about my body and my fitness journey. As one of my health coaches said, "There is no time for self-deprecation in reaching goals." So I need to catch myself when I am starting to tell myself things like:

You'll never be able to do this.
Your body is just not meant to be this size/weight.

STOP! Nope! There's no time for that kind of thinking here.

I am worth it.
I am worth the time and effort that it will take me to reach this goal.

Those positive thoughts feel a little more authentic and supportive of what I need to get through this hurdle.

Empathize
Validate
Support

These are the three things I need to give myself on a regular basis so I can better show up for the people in my life that I love.

So when my daughter comes home from school upset about something that happened in her day, I need to help her name her feelings. I need to tell her that I understand how she feels. Then, I need to ask her what she needs from me. Maybe she doesn't need a list of solutions. Maybe she simply needs me to sit with her, listen, let her cry, give her hugs...and just make space for her and what she is going through.

See...when we can do this for ourselves, it is much easier to do this for others. I may be a Social Emotional Learning Coach, but I still struggle with my emotions. Being human isn't easy—we have a lot of thoughts, judgments, and preconceived notions floating around inside our brains. And just like the rest of the human race, I am learning too.

It is important to encourage ourselves to express thoughts and emotions without the fear of judgment.

That way, we can give the people we love space to express their thoughts and emotions without fear of judgment.

To my friend who pointed out her annoyance at my positivity, I get it! And I'm learning from what you expressed to me. And to my student who got me to reflect on the emotions I struggle with...thank you! I really needed that...and so did my daughter!

CHAPTER 45

nature can nurture

THIS YEAR, I SET A GOAL FOR MYSELF TO GET BACK INTO working in schools again. My heart is in a school building, working with teachers, students, staff, and administrators. I know firsthand how challenging working in classrooms can be. The rewards, while they are tremendous, can sometimes feel out of reach. I know that, as a public school classroom teacher, I often felt overwhelmed and exhausted. But at the same time, I felt excited and inspired. The emotional rollercoaster of one school day is truly incredible. It takes a strong ability for educators to use emotion regulation tools in order to manage it all! And as I know firsthand, using these tools isn't always seamless!

I am excited to say that I'm doing it! I am working in schools, running wellness workshops, and collaborating with educators. I share tools that teachers and staff can use to help their own social and emotional well-being and share with their students.

So yay! I am taking a moment in this story to celebrate! I feel proud! I feel excited! I am feeling successful in my goals and intentions for this fairly new path in which I find myself walking!

Lately, I remembered something about myself that I've known for a while:

I like routine and structure.
I like lists.
I like to check off items on my lists.
I like schedules.

And when I feel off a routine, off-schedule, or I can't complete my to-do list...I feel stressed and overwhelmed. So, while I feel excited to get back into working in schools, I feel worried about my goals and intentions for this next chapter in my career.

Let me explain...

Writing wellness workshops for educators takes a lot of time and creativity. Talking to interested schools, learning about their needs, remembering my feelings when I was in the classroom, knowing what children face in school every day, and then creating a workshop that I think will be entertaining and valuable for educators *is hard work*.

Once I create a workshop, I need to advertise it. Then, once a school is interested, I need to practice and build enough confidence in myself to make an engaging presentation for an audience that doesn't know me from a hole in the wall.

I am learning and creating at the same time. And while it feels incredibly pleasant to follow my dreams, goals, and intentions...it can also feel incredibly nerve-wracking! My to-do list builds and builds, and then suddenly, I feel like I don't have enough time.

I started to notice an increase in my pace of life in the last week or two. The list of things I needed and wanted to do got incredibly long. I began working at night and over the weekends. I also noticed that all of this work and thinking about work was leaving me distracted. I wasn't entirely listening to my family when they told me stories at dinner. I was late for things. I wasn't reading my emails carefully, so I missed details and dates. I felt out of control, off my routine, and unable to keep up.

I am so glad I noticed these feelings bubbling up inside me. My stress response has always been the same...*the way I combat feeling overwhelmed is to make myself a list and work on a little bit at a time.* And then I proceed to use every free minute I have to do it all! This impacts my sleep and my ability to be present.

I know perfectly well that I don't have to respond to this new-found work stress in this way. Making a list is good for getting everything I have to do out of my head and keeping myself organized so I don't miss anything. The only problem with that is that I wasn't thinking about blocking any time out to take care of myself in this busy schedule. Everything on the list pertained to what work and my family needed. And by the start of this week, I knew this pace would not be sustainable.

I know that I cannot take care of anyone or anything else unless I make sure my needs are met, too.

So...what did I do? Good question....

The first thing I did was ask myself how I was feeling. I preach this a lot...name it to tame it. Or feel it to heal it. At the pace I was running, I wasn't taking the time to notice that I was feeling irritable and cranky because I was exhausted, overwhelmed, and nervous. Once I was able to label these feelings, I knew exactly what I needed.

I was craving fresh air.
I wanted to move.
I desired a slower pace.

Notice I didn't say that I needed a cocktail, a pedicure, a shopping spree, or a bubble bath?! While those things are lovely, they weren't going to fulfill my needs. And I never would have known that if I didn't first stop and ask myself how I was feeling. But our culture will tell us that when we are feeling stressed...

Have a drink.
Go to the spa.
Do some retail therapy.

But those things weren't going to give me the fresh air, movement, or slower pace that I knew would help me.

So, I decided to make it my intention to go outside for a walk this week. Just one walk. If I could do more than that, BONUS! I looked at my schedule and the weather (it is winter in New England, after all) and decided that I would go for a walk after the kids went to school this morning and before I started to tackle my to-do list.

I did everything I could to set myself up for success and not succumb to all the things I knew I had to do. I took my workout clothes out of my drawers so they were visible when I woke up this morning. I put my sneakers, winter hat, and gloves near the door. I cued up a playlist on Spotify, and I set a reminder on my calendar to take a walk. I had no excuses.

So I did it!
I walked for forty minutes.
In the cold air.
Down to the beach in my neighborhood and back.
And it was glorious!

I didn't even think about working up a sweat. I forgot to turn on my Spotify playlist. As soon as the fresh air hit my lungs, I knew I made the right choice.

While I walked, I noticed so many beautiful things...there wasn't a breath of air, so the water down at the beach reflected the land around it. I was the only one by the shore, but there were footprints in the sand, so I knew that there were others who were enjoying this beautiful morning as well! I noticed little fishing and quahogging boats dotting the horizon. The clouds made beautiful colors and patterns in the sky. Even the dying dune grass looked gorgeous along the blues and grays of the water and the space around it. I giggled at the seagulls (which I usually find annoying) squawking at each other while they waded in the freezing cold water. As I circled back home, I enjoyed the sight of several bright red cardinals and their mates in the leaf-less trees.

I have no idea how fast or how far I walked. It didn't matter. I gave myself exactly what I needed…fresh air in my lungs and on my skin, movement, and a slower pace to notice the beauty around me. The time I gave myself this morning slowed me down enough to remember that connection with nature is important, even in the dead of winter. And since the beach is my favorite place on Earth, it is no wonder that my feet took me in that direction.

I am sitting here thinking, "where would I be right now if I didn't take that walk this morning?" A few more items on my to-do list would have been checked off than there are right now. I'd probably be showered. But I would still be in my own hurricane of unpleasant emotions, sitting in my typical stress response state that I know I don't like and doesn't serve me.

Instead, I am feeling confident. I am feeling proud of myself. And I am feeling relaxed. It is amazing what one little change in my approach to my day can do for my mindset.

So here I am…writing this story, still in my workout clothes, and it is already 10:30 in the morning. My kids went to school almost two hours ago, and time is flying! Writing this story was on my to-do list, but after the walk I took this morning, it doesn't feel like work. It doesn't feel overwhelming to write. Because of the time I gave to my needs this morning, I am working more efficiently and effortlessly. I know that the other twenty-five things on my list to do today will get done. And if they don't?! There's always tomorrow, and that is OK.

CHAPTER 46

white picket fences around me

BRENÉ BROWN IS LEGENDARY. SHE IS A PROFESSOR, author of numerous books, and podcast host. Listening to her TED talks makes me feel like I can take on the world. She doles out self-help like candy. I am mesmerized by her messages of empathy, vulnerability, shame, and courage. When I think about my day-to-day balance of life and career, I often ask myself, "What would Brené say to me right now?"

It is September, and many of us are sending our children back to school. Teachers and families are fully immersed in the chaos, stress, and joy that this time of year can bring. This is why it is time to talk about what I call our "white picket fences." Do you know what these are? These fences do exactly what they are set up to do—create a boundary between you and the rest of the world!

"Daring to set boundaries is about having the courage to love ourselves even when we risk disappointing others."
—*Brené Brown*

I like to imagine the boundaries I set as white picket fences, the quintessential image of a beautiful suburban neighborhood. They aren't stockade fences that prevent me from seeing beyond the boundary. They aren't chain link fences that keep me in like a prisoner. They are pretty and clean-looking, maybe lined with flowers and cute little shrubs. I can see over them. I can see through them. But yet, they create a boundary between me and the rest of the world. While this may deter people from crossing into my space, it doesn't create a feeling of unwelcome or prevent people from visiting me from the other side.

Setting boundaries protects my peace. I have spent countless hours dreaming about how I would like to spend my time. It is so easy for teachers and parents to lose hours of their lives to their jobs. However, too much time spent working, grading, and planning can lead to faster burnout and lower quality of work.

I wish someone had given me the following advice in the early days of my career:

A White Picket Fence Around Time Outside the Office/Classroom:

- Many of us don't have the luxury of leaving our work behind at the office. We often take it home, invading our family and personal time. The best way to manage this is to block out a couple of hours outside of your work time to complete what needs to get done. Work your heart out during the time you've blocked off, but then wrap it up. Put everything back into your work bag and stick to that time frame. On the rare occasion when you have less work to do, use that time to get ahead if needed.
- Get picky about the work you are doing after work

hours. Ask yourself, What will happen if this work isn't done by tomorrow? Is that result worth giving up my personal and family time? If I don't do this work tonight/over the weekend, will I spend my downtime worrying about it? Then, choose what work to complete and the time frame in which you've set, and go from there. Stay on track and consistent, but put a time limit on this work and save the rest for tomorrow.

- For many years, I taught in the same town where I lived. This was tricky! My family often called me "the mayor" because we couldn't go anywhere without someone saying hello to me and stopping me to have a chat. This often happened at the grocery store, while I was out to dinner with my family, or even at other school events for my own children! A great boundary I learned I had to build was to never discuss school or business in public. I often ran into parents, students, co-workers, PTO members, admins, school district employees, and more! They wanted to stop and chat about an issue they were seeing with their child in school, a question they had about something going on in my classroom, or a concern they had over a test grade. It was always an awkward moment when I had to say, "Send me an email or give me a call on Monday. We can talk about it then." This may have turned some people off, but it got my needs met, which was most important. And when they did follow up with an email, I NEVER apologized for being unable to talk to them out in public. I simply thanked them for waiting and getting in contact with me at a more appropriate time.

A White Picket Fence Around Taking Breaks:

- As a teacher and/or a parent, it is so easy to get lost in all you have to do. Find time in your day for yourself and protect that time like a precious baby. Take non-negotiable and scheduled breaks for yourself throughout your day. A break will make you better able to tackle whatever comes up through the rest of your day. There are so many ways you can schedule these breaks. For example, consciously choose to step away from your desk or out of your classroom at lunchtime. Make a plan to eat with a colleague or join others in the teacher's room. Choose one of your planning periods a week or block a bit of time each week to spend alone. Close your classroom or office door. Listen to some music or a podcast. Put on your coat and go outside for a walk. Do whatever you need to do to take a break from the hectic nature of your work day.
- Feeling sick? Stay home and rest. Need a mental health day? Take it. If you aren't feeling yourself, you will never perform at your best. And honestly, you will just make yourself feel worse. If you are a parent and/or a teacher, chances are you are taking loving care of everyone around you. You deserve that same loving care when you need it, too.

A White Picket Fence Around Saying "No"

- One of the best pieces of advice that I got from an unofficial teaching mentor was, "No is a complete sentence." It isn't a bad word. It isn't something to apologize for saying. It is hard and scary to use at first, but it gets easier, and you will thank yourself for using it. You can say no when your principal asks you to be on a committee after school hours. You can say no to the PTO when they ask you to be a speaker at their next meeting. You can say no to students when they ask for a "make-your-own-slime day," and you're not up for it. You can say no to a colleague or parent who asks for "just five minutes" when they haven't pre-scheduled a meeting with you.

One of the reasons it is hard to build these white picket fences is because a majority of us are selfless and giving people. Especially as educators and parents, we may feel it is our duty to be nurturers and to sacrifice our time and needs for the safety and security of others. There have been times I've felt that I'm not good enough unless I'm giving it all I've got until I've got nothing left. There is a saying that states,

> "What you allow, will continue."

Knowing this, I began to ask myself, "Do I really want to continue on this path of self-destruction? Would I want to see your loved ones do this to themselves?"

We have to speak up for our needs as human beings because no one else will do that for us. Not because we are lazy. Not because we don't care. Although, our society may try to sell it that way. We can build a happy little white picket fence for ourselves because we recognize our worth as a person who was made not only for service to others but to experience peace and joy in life!

Learning to create and stick to boundaries takes a lot of courage. It is a growth process that won't happen overnight. You will cave and will have to start over. You will feel a lot of guilt in these moments.

However, ultimately, you will gain self-confidence and be an even better person, partner, teacher, employee, and parent than you ever dreamed you could be! You will have the energy to focus on the things that matter in your classroom, your office, your home, and in your life.

...and if it makes you feel better to be more polite, you can always say, "No, thanks."

CHAPTER 47

kickboxing is my anger management

EXERCISE IS A TOOL FOR ME THAT I USE DAILY. AS MANY of you know, I like to run. My knees don't like it, but it is a tool to help me with a number of things in life. First off, it helps me connect. I have two friends that I run with regularly. At 5:15 a.m., we decorate ourselves like Christmas trees, with lights and reflectors, and meet out on the street to hit the pavement. The fresh (and sometimes downright cold) air in my lungs, combined with the movement, starts my day off right. Not only is running a tool to connect me with friends, but it is a stress relief. On days that I meet my friends for a run, my head is clear, and I feel like I can take on anything that comes my way. Running brings me patience, which, as a teacher and mom, I desperately need!

I also like to lift weights. This is a new exercise for me that I have only really discovered recently. This is a tool that not only keeps me strong but also helps me lose weight. In the last eight months or so since I have adopted three days a week of lifting weights, I have lost almost thirty pounds. This is an incredible tool for my physical health, and we all know the powerful connection between physical and mental well-being.

Yoga is a grounding tool for me. This regular movement gives me the ability to connect with myself and find my peace. Without this tool, I wouldn't be able to lead my students from a place of calm. Connecting my breath with movement helps me to get into my own head and body, checking out from the constant stress of the outside world. I am able to leave everything that I experienced throughout the day outside of the room, get on my mat, and focus on myself.

As a Social-Emotional Learning coach, I work with kids, their families, and teachers to handle all emotions that come our way as humans. I am always modeling breathwork and meditation, and I wonder if my clients know that I am not always the calm and peaceful person they see in our sessions every week. Sometimes, I struggle with big and unpleasant emotions, and there isn't enough running, weight lifting, or yoga to manage it.

Which is why I started kickboxing.

You heard me right...I wrap my hands, strap on some gloves, turn on ridiculously loud music, and kick the heck out of my anger of the moment. And let me tell you, these days, I've been pretty angry.

I am angry at politics.

I am angry at the hatred and the fighting happening in our world today.

I am angry at the guy who just gave me the finger on the highway.

I am angry at the receptionist at the dentist's office who called me "ma'am" in a really condescending way.

I am angry that my Jewish friends are afraid to worship at their temple or send their children to Hebrew School.

I am angry that I ran over a screw and gave myself a flat tire.

I am angry that my kids and their classmates can't go to school without the fear of an attack.

I am angry that I went out to lunch with friends yesterday, and it took close to an hour to get our food delivered to the table.

I am angry that I can't turn on the news without hearing about someone being killed, tortured, or abused.

I am angry that there are people out there who don't believe in global warming.

I am angry that the grocery store messed up my "Drive Up and Go" order.

I am just plain angry sometimes...and that's OK.

That's why I kickbox. As soon as the music starts to blare, I throw some punches, and I throw them hard. I kick the bag and find satisfaction in the sound of my foot making contact. I sweat. I swear loudly because no one can hear me over the music anyway. I literally pay someone to let me hurt the poor bag that is taking a beating for all the anger that I have pent up inside of me.

I think if my students and their families came to watch me kickbox, they wouldn't recognize me. I am always surprising my kids' friends when they see my gloves in the back seat of my car. I find that a good thing! Because without kickboxing, I wouldn't have a tool to get it all out. I would hate to think of where my anger would be released. When I get on the kickboxing mat, I can have an imaginary brawl with whatever and whoever is pissing me off at the moment. After about an hour, when I am sweaty and spent, I go home, take a shower, and feel a bit lighter. My anger has been released, and I can find space for the emotions I find much more pleasant.

Like Rocky Balboa so famously said,

> "It ain't about how hard you can hit. It's about how hard you can get hit and keep moving forward."

You see, all the things that make me angry are just life's punches that keep getting thrown at me. Some of those punches hit me hard. But having a tool to release the emotion that comes with those punches helps me to move forward. And I am able to move forward to a place where I can help others, lead, and share love. In other words, kickboxing helps me be the teacher, the parent, and the person that most people recognize...the calm, loving, peaceful me instead of the kickboxing lunatic working out to inappropriately loud music.

And the bonus? All these exercises are not only a tool to help me manage my emotions. It also gives me mad muscles, which makes me feel strong. And I like that!

CHAPTER 48

name it to tame it

I'VE BEEN FEELING A LITTLE DOWN LATELY. MAYBE "down" isn't the right word to describe how I'm feeling. I have a mixture of different emotions going on right now.

> Maybe I'm a little worried.
> I might be a tiny bit sad.
> I could be slightly overwhelmed.
> ...or deflated, uneasy, and spent.

Wow...that's a lot of unpleasant emotions happening all at once! But that's not all that I'm feeling. I have a few pleasant emotions swirling around, too.

> I'm definitely content.
> I might be a little proud.
> I am fully feeling grateful.
> ...or focused, secure, and satisfied.

You're probably wondering how I can feel all that at the same time! Well...I believe it is called "the human experience." And in order to fully feel and be present in our lives, we have to acknowledge and move through it all.

> We cannot selectively numb emotions.
> When we numb the painful emotions, we also numb the positive emotions.
> —*Brené Brown*

Thanks, Brené, but I think this is a lot easier said than done. Would you agree? It is so much easier for me to focus on the pleasant emotions and push those unpleasant ones way down deep.

Notice I use the language "pleasant and unpleasant" rather than "positive and negative" when talking about emotions. I try really hard to follow Marc Brackett's thinking. Marc expressed this exact sentiment when attending a RULER training a few years ago. He taught me that there is nothing **wrong** with feeling unpleasant feelings and nothing **right** about feeling pleasant ones. Emotions are simply data that tell us what might be going on with us right now. And if we listen to the emotions swirling around inside of us, both pleasant and unpleasant, we can decide how we want to manage those feelings.

So, let's go back to my ease in pushing unpleasant emotions way down deep. From my experience, I've discovered that it only works for a short amount of time before things explode. For example, nothing drives me more crazy than frustration over shoes in my house. How is it possible that four people have two hundred and fifty-two pairs of shoes, all sitting at the front door, ready to put on our feet as we're walking out?

Every day, I walk into my house, usually with my arms full, and trip over the shoes in the doorway into my home. I feel frustrated by the fact that these shoes greet me and trip me almost every day.

Often, I drop my things on the counter and go back to the shoes, organizing them into a place where no one will trip on them and making things look a little neater at the entrance to our home.

About twenty minutes later, the shoes are strewn around the front door again, guaranteed. My frustration mounts when it continues to happen several times a day, almost every day. And as that frustration grows, so does my anger until the final time when I walk in the door and trip on a pair of shoes. I scream and yell my head off at the first family member I see. Suddenly, everyone comes running to fix the shoes, apologizing and walking on eggshells for me. That is, until the next day, when the shoes are back there again, ready for me to trip and fall on at any moment.

These are not my finest minutes. I'm not proud of myself when I walk in the door like a "Screaming Meemie," seeing my kids with a panic-stricken look on their faces as I yell at them. If I could give myself a do-over in these moments, I would go back to the first time I walked into the house, tripping over the thousands of shoes in the doorway. I would put my things down and take a breath. I would notice that I am feeling frustrated and name those feelings in my mind. I would take a few minutes to unpack my belongings before reacting to this situation. I would also notice that I was feeling excited to come home and begin my time with my family, recognizing pleasant and unpleasant feelings existing together at the same time.

So as not to ruin the excitement that I felt when I walked in the door, I would find my family and gather them together. As calmly as possible, I would share that I often walk in the door with an arm full of belongings, tripping over the shoes. I would express that this makes me feel frustrated, and I would ask them for help in cleaning and organizing the shoes, being more mindful of where the shoes are placed when they come home. I may also ask them to take some shoes that they don't wear regularly and put them away in the closet.

I know perfectly well that if I acknowledge my unpleasant feelings and decide the best way to express them, it will not ruin the pleasant feelings that I also have swirling around inside me. By suppressing my frustration and allowing it to bubble up over time, exploding with anger, I robbed myself of enjoying the evening with my family, which I was looking forward to and feeling excited about.

This seems very simple, doesn't it? But this gets harder when the emotions are even more raw than frustration over shoes in the doorway. The death of a loved one, receiving devastating news about your health, losing your job...any part of the human experience that may bring you pain can make it hard to allow ourselves to feel. We often turn to other things to help dull our feelings. Some turn to alcohol or drugs. Others may turn to shopping, gambling, or scrolling on their phone. We think that these things will help us feel better. But there's a problem that lies in this kind of thinking.

> This implies that better = good.
> ...that feeling better will make you feel "good."
> But feeling "good" will only be temporary.

What if we thought about healing instead of feeling "better." When we feel better after a cold or the flu, aren't we healed? In order to heal and feel the full spectrum of emotion, we must allow ourselves to feel the unpleasant feelings so we don't rob ourselves of the things that heal us in our lives, too.

I invite you to think about what medicine you can find around you that helps you heal. Is it nature? Do you feel calm and balanced when you sit by the ocean or take a walk through the trees?

Sometimes, sitting in quiet and stillness can bring healing. Maybe reading a book, meditating, or snuggling up with a pet can be just the medicine you need.

For some, spending time with friends and loved ones can be healing. Processing the emotions with your support system by having others hear you, laugh with you, and cry along with you can be very soothing.

Research says that labeling our emotions, especially unpleasant ones, can help us create distance between ourselves and our experience, allowing us to choose how to respond to challenges. In fact, research at UCLA calls verbal labeling of emotions "affect labeling." These researchers have brain scan data to show that practicing affect labeling appears to decrease activity in the brain's emotional centers, including the amygdala, allowing the brain's frontal lobe (the center for reasoning and thinking) to have greater sway over solving problems at hand.

So, what's the bottom line? I'm giving myself (and you!) permission to *feel all the feels*. There's nothing bad about feeling worried, sad, overwhelmed, or frustrated. I don't need to ignore or judge those feelings because, without them, I won't feel all those pleasant feelings I have, too! I enjoy feeling content, proud, grateful, and secure. Without my pleasant feelings, there would be no healing. And who wants to live in a world like that?

CHAPTER 49

practice makes progress

A FEW WEEKS AGO, ONE OF MY STUDENTS SHOWED UP in tears for their session. She refused to get out of the car, closing the door every time her mother tried to open it. She was clearly feeling something unpleasant and high energy...was it anger? Frustration? Nervousness?

I didn't know what transpired moments before she arrived at my office, so I didn't know the trigger for her unpleasant emotions. All I knew was what was happening right in front of me, and it was clear that she was not in the headspace to do what I had planned that afternoon.

Isn't that the way with education? In a classroom of over twenty students, there is bound to be a student or two who is not ready to receive the lesson you had planned. They need time to process a big emotion they may be feeling or an event that happened before your class started. And you may not always understand what triggered the unpleasant emotions.

Isn't that the way with parenting, too? Sometimes, when I pick my child up from school or practice, they aren't in the mood to tell me about their day or do an errand that I need to do before we get home. They might be feeling tired from a long day at school or tough practice. Or they might be feeling something else pretty big. They need time to unwind and take a breath before they are off to the next thing.

So how do we manage this? I have a suggestion....

Co-regulation.

Co-regulating with a child isn't easy; it takes time, and for some of you out there, it might sound a little hokey. We often hear about co-regulation as something you do with a baby. When a baby is fussing, parents are often encouraged to pick them up, hug them, and tell them through facial expressions and tone of voice that everything is going to be OK. And they keep doing that until they calm down. The hard part about co-regulating with infants is finding what works. And what helps soothe a baby today might not work tomorrow.

It isn't often that we hear about co-regulation with humans of all ages. However, there is research out there that says that co-regulating can help humans learn to regulate their emotions, and it works in a similar way as it does with infants. Sometimes, co-regulation with older kids can start with a hug, a squeeze, and some other sort of physical connection. Sometimes, it doesn't have to include any of that. Soft tones of voice and calm facial expressions are essential, however, to help a child move through the big emotion they may be feeling.

Let's go back to my student who arrived for their session emotionally dysregulated. Tensions were high for everyone involved. I could tell her mom was possibly feeling a little embarrassed, frustrated, or even angry. I was feeling a little unsure if there was anything I could do to help, but I decided to give it a try anyway.

I calmly walked over to the car and opened the door. I tried to make my facial expression appear relaxed and understanding. I squatted down at the open door so that I could look eye-to-eye with my student sitting in the car. Then, in a very soothing tone of voice, I told them that I could tell they were feeling something unpleasant. I explained that I didn't know what happened and I didn't need to know, but I was there to help. In as little language as possible, I told my student that they didn't need to do anything that they weren't comfortable with and invited them to see if they could listen to my breathing. I began to take deep breaths. She started to cry a little louder, but I remained calm but persistent.

Although it took time, she eventually started to listen to my breathing.

When I noticed that her tears began to subside and her breathing became more regular, I invited her to try to match my breathing. At first, she just stared at me.

But I kept going.

She was getting more calm with every breath I took.

And eventually, she started to join me.

The whole thing took less than ten minutes. I didn't do a lot of talking. I didn't get too much into her feelings. I just breathed, and she was willing to follow along. When I saw that her flushed face faded and the tears slowed down, I asked her if she wanted to come inside to play a game or make a craft rather than do our lesson. Miraculously, she agreed to follow me in.

Eventually, during a little bit of clay-creating, my student was able to tell me how she was feeling before we started our session. We didn't get to do all I planned for our afternoon, but we eventually got into most of it, which made me feel like the mission was accomplished. In all honesty, I think my student learned more from the co-regulating experience than she would have from my lesson anyway.

And all it took was a little breathing together.

Can you imagine if teachers co-regulated with their students in the classroom? It might not look like the moment I had with my student, but it could have the same theme. The teacher could lead some breathing exercises, giving students the option to listen along or join in. Maybe classroom lights could be dimmed, and the teacher could consciously keep their voice calm. Maybe they get their students' attention with a soft chime or some other signal to quiet down. Perhaps an adult in the building takes individual students in need for a walk or to a quiet place to sit.

This sounds pretty simple on paper, but I know perfectly well that in a public school, this isn't easy....

Co-regulating takes time.
Time away from academics.
Time to get students who live in a very fast-paced world to be comfortable with slowing down.
Time that public schools don't *really* have.

Can you also imagine if parents co-regulated with their children at home? It won't look anything like it would in a classroom, but it could be similar to what I did with my student...getting down to a child's level to look eye-to-eye with them, using as little language as possible, using a quiet tone of voice, and starting with a tool, like breathing, that they could use in an attempt to regulate their big feelings.

Again, this sounds pretty simple, but as a parent, I know this isn't easy. We have our own feelings about the situation.

Co-regulating takes patience.
Patience to move through our own big emotions while helping regulate our child's.
Patience to let our child move through their emotions at their own pace.
Patience that parents don't *always* have!

Breathing is just one tool for co-regulating, and what a teacher or a parent tries today might not work tomorrow. But that is OK. It is a start. It is also a way to teach children emotion regulation tools through modeling. When a child is feeling dysregulated, it is hard for them to access the tools that work for them. Sometimes, they need an adult to do it with them.

A few days after my session with this student, I got a text from her mom with a story that she just couldn't wait to share with me. Her mom explained that the day before, she was having a bad day. Work was rough, the drive home was challenging, and nothing seemed to be going her way. The last straw for her was when she dropped and broke a glass on the floor after dinner. Her daughter found her on the floor and in tears as she cleaned up the mess. When she was finished, her daughter sat on the couch with her and, without much talk, took her hand and invited her mother to breathe with her.

Her daughter was trying to co-regulate with her.
Without even really understanding what that was.
And her mother was so grateful for this new tool.

This kind of stuff doesn't happen overnight. And some nights it doesn't work at all. But with consistency, patience, and practice, we can all get there. The key is remembering that practice ***doesn't make perfect***...it makes ***progress,*** and that is all we can ask for, right?

CHAPTER 50

just lose that narrative

YOU KNOW GEORGE ORWELL, RIGHT? ONE THING YOU may not know about me is that I had a double major in college—Elementary Education and English. I had to read *a lot* back in school. And George Orwell's work stuck with me. That is his pen name, however. He is also known as Eric Arthur Blair. He was an English author known for his novels *1984* and *Animal Farm*, both of which many of you probably read in school. He once wrote,

> "If thought corrupts language, language can also corrupt thought."

I think what he means by this is that the more we use poor language, the poorer our thoughts become. I was reminded of this by someone a few days ago.

I am a social being. As a kid and young adult, I really enjoyed being part of something. I was involved in so many different clubs and sports...swimming, sailing, the school newspaper, theater, and track! If something looked interesting to me, I had no problems diving in head first to try it out. And I loved meeting new people!

As an adult, not much of that about me has changed. I thrive on being surrounded by a community, which is why I am struggling in this "newish" role that I find myself in! I have my own business. I work from home. I don't have colleagues to bounce ideas off of, learn from, and chat with.

That is why I was excited to meet my new friend, Lauren! We weren't complete strangers. I learned about her through LinkedIn. She is the owner of her own coaching business, so of course, I immediately became interested in what she had to say. She posts inspiring quotes and stories of her own life that resonate with me. I have enjoyed following her journey into motherhood and business ownership but have never actually talked to her in real life. Isn't it funny how social media can make us feel connected even when we're really not?

Anyway, I posted something on LinkedIn about Calm Education, and Lauren liked it. Nothing about this was new. I've noticed that we alternately give each other positive feedback about each other's posts through a "thumbs-up" or a "heart." The difference in this feedback was that a mutual friend (who I actually know in real life!) noticed the connection and asked me how I knew Lauren. When I expressed that I didn't really know her, the response was, "Do you want me to introduce you?" And of course, the answer was YES!

A few days later, I found myself enjoying a cup of coffee on a virtual sit-down with Lauren. She initiated the meeting, and I was delighted to meet her in "person." We shared about our journeys into the roles we have taken on and the trials and tribulations of business ownership. But there was something really meaningful that I got from our conversation that I feel I need to share.

Lauren previously worked in the business world. She shared her feelings about working in a world full of hustling and her uncertainty about whether this world was good for her well-being and her family. As an educator, I could completely relate! My response to her was something along the lines of, "I wasn't like you. I was *just* a teacher. But I can relate to the feeling of uncertainty around a job that was starting to affect my well-being."

In the most gentle and loving way, she stopped me in my tracks by saying, "I've heard you call yourself *just* a teacher a few times in this conversation. You need to change that narrative. My daughter's teachers are part of my village, and I need them. Teachers aren't *just* anything."

She was right, and boy, was I glad that she called me on that one. I haven't been able to stop thinking about it. How many times have I said I am *just* a teacher? *Just* a mom? *Just* a beginner business owner? There is so much meaning behind that one little four-letter j-word! It simplifies what I am. It downplays how I identify. It belittles what I do. And that is not OK.

I am sharing this story with you in the hopes that you can learn from my conversation with Lauren. Many of you out there are also teachers and parents. There is nothing simple about what it takes to step into those roles. You raise and mold the future. You welcome all types, inspire curiosity, resolve conflicts, scatter kindness, demonstrate problem-solving, and lead from love (*just* to name a few things...)! And you do this in times of chaos, excitement, and stress. You aren't *just* part of the village. You ARE the village. And that is enough! You are enough!

Educators don't always walk around in high-powered suits. They don't always drive fancy cars and never get to take long, boozy lunches. They're lucky to get twenty minutes to use the restroom and scarf down last night's leftovers during their lunch break! There is nothing glamorous about teaching and parenting. Society has created a narrative that to be enough, we have to have something to show for it. It is hard to quantitatively show our place in the village. Is that why we are "just" something?

Catch yourself the next time you hear yourself using that word, and remind yourself that the inner critic is not invited to your village. Take a nice, deep breath and correct yourself. You aren't JUST anything. Saying that word is using poor language and creating even poorer thoughts in your mind and those around you. You are amazing. You are important. You are needed. You are enough!

And thank you, Lauren, for that reminder. I am forever grateful, and I can't wait to see where our friendship goes!

CHAPTER 51

practicing positivity

AS MANY OF YOU KNOW, I AM A FORMER PUBLIC school teacher. I have so many memories of those years...time spent with my students, and the connections I made! I have heaps of stories that will make you both laugh and cry, sometimes at the same time!

One story I am going to tell today is about one of the most memorable starts of a school year. Many public schools in New England start in the last week of August when it is hot, muggy, and humid! But this particular morning wasn't like that. I remember because a fellow teacher friend of mine and I decided to go for an early morning jog before meeting our students for the first time. It was a slightly cool morning...one of those mornings where it was somewhat chilly to start, but you knew the day would get warmer by the minute. We had an enjoyable run together, chatting the entire time and working to burn off the nerves we felt over starting a new school year. We ran together just as the sun was rising in the sky. I'll never forget that it was a gorgeous start to the day.

But that wasn't the excitement of the morning. The excitement started when I got to school! After our run, I showered and put on a new summer dress that I picked out, especially for the occasion. I ate breakfast and packed my first bagged lunch of the school year. Then I was off! I drove into the parking lot of my school, grabbed my belongings, and walked into the building. The floors looked shiny and newly waxed. Signs welcomed parents and students back to school. I could tell everyone was ready! I was one of the first teachers to arrive, and I didn't see a single soul in sight. So, I walked down the hallway toward my classroom. As I rounded the corner, I heard a splash and noticed a wet sensation at my feet. I was standing in a few inches of water!!

This realization didn't make sense to me. Why was I wading in water? I looked down the hallway and realized that water was flowing in my direction. Was I imagining this? No one was here to witness what I was seeing.

I decided to walk back to where I came from, to drier ground. I looked around for someone to tell, but there was no one. So I called my friend that I had run with earlier in the morning…she hadn't arrived at school yet. One hallway of the school was flooding, and students, parents, and teachers were on their way to start a new school year! This couldn't be happening.…

It turns out that a pipe broke from a sink in the custodian's closet. Water flowed for a while into classrooms and down the hallways. The water was stopped but not cleaned up before students began arriving at school a few moments later. Our principal and teachers scrambled to figure out what to do with the displaced classrooms on that side of the building.

We all went into "go mode," gathering all the supplies we could from our soggy classrooms and directing students to meet us in the cafeteria. We each found a corner of the school building to work or a stretch of space outside where we could read, talk, and try to make the first day of school a little fun for our students. We moved around all day long, working where we could.

When the students left for the day, I was exhausted (to say the least). I also felt stressed, overwhelmed, and uncertain about how the school would continue with wet and soggy classrooms. So many things went wrong....

My students never saw their classroom on the first day of school.

Everything that I set up for my students in the room was ruined by water.

Supplies that I used regularly, some of which I paid for with my own money, had to be thrown away.

The school had to close for a few days, and we were required to help with the clean-up effort.

They had to cut the walls of our classrooms to dry out and replace them in order to prevent mold from growing.

This was the all-time worst first day of school I ever had! I felt like crying, and I had to do a lot to keep my emotions in check that day and the days that followed in the clean-up effort. All of my emotion regulation tools came out in full force!

I'll never forget standing in my classroom with a big trash bag and throwing out wet books. My heart was breaking as I threw away things that meant something to me and the items that I knew I wouldn't have for my new students.

At one point, another colleague came into my room with tears in her eyes. She expressed that she was exhausted, overwhelmed, and angry about the whole thing. I listened and empathized. I felt the same way. But then, I expressed to her...

No one got hurt.

Books, furniture, materials, and even walls can be replaced.

None of this will matter in a few short weeks.

We did the best we could, considering the circumstances!

The response from my colleague was one I will never forget. She said to me, "How do you always stay so positive?"

This question stopped me in my tracks. POSITIVE? I responded, "I'm not! Trust me...I'm thinking all sorts of negative things right now. But they aren't helping me move forward."

This wasn't the first time I had been called out on my positivity. Usually, people call it out when they are finding it hard to be positive. They are either annoyed by me or trying to seek positive vibes in hopes they rub off on them.

But see...that's the thing. I don't think I can call myself a positive person. I am human. I have negative thoughts, just like the rest of them. Anyone who says they are positive all the time HAS to be lying.

I'm not a positive person.
I practice positivity.

Sometimes we, as humans, get sucked into thinking about what is wrong, what's not working, and what could be better. Sometimes, we get caught in a cycle of complaining. It happens! But awareness of getting caught in a "stinking thinking" loop is the first step toward practicing positivity.

Positivity is an attitude that affects how we experience ourselves, others, and our situations. It also affects how we behave. Winston Churchill said that,

> "A pessimist sees the difficulty in every opportunity; an optimist sees the opportunity in every difficulty."

When we are positive, the glass is half-full rather than half-empty. Practicing positivity means trying to be optimistic and hopeful rather than negative and hopeless. When we practice positivity, we look at a world full of opportunities to make things better rather than a world full of problems. In the practice of positivity, humans focus on what they are grateful for, their blessings, and the good in life rather than what they don't have and what is wrong. Sometimes, when we practice positivity, we realize that what first seemed like a problem really isn't a big deal after all!

When it comes down to it, positive people attract other positive people and participate in positive activities. Since they put out a positive attitude into the world and do positive things, positivity comes back to them over and over again.

I want that.
That world seems WAY more attractive to me.
So, I work really hard to practice positivity.

Is this practice of being positive with both ourselves and others seamless and easy? NOPE. I have to work at it. Being aware and mindful of my thoughts and the things I say out loud is the very beginning.

When I notice that my thoughts and things I say to others start with "I can't" or "I'll never," I take a pause. I don't criticize myself for thinking this way; I just simply notice my negative self-talk and try to reframe it to something that is a little more kind or supportive. While I know that I have weaknesses and faults, I try to focus on leveraging my strengths and talents instead. When I encounter defeat, I try not to let myself be defeated.

I also try really hard to express my gratitude for everything and everyone that surrounds me. I list these things in my regular meditation practice and write them in my journal. And when I am feeling grateful to someone, I say it directly to them as much as possible! Expressing everything I am grateful for helps to put me in a more positive frame of mind.

When I am having a particularly rough day, I try to pause, notice, and release judgment on that, too! These are the days when I may try to be a little extra kind to myself and take the time to do something that makes me feel happy. Usually, these are also the times that I notice that I haven't been doing these things for myself as much as I should! But sometimes, it even feels better on these tough days to do something nice for someone else. I'll buy a coffee for the person behind me in line, text a friend and tell them something I appreciate about them, or send someone a card...these acts of kindness often take me out of my negatively clouded head to a more grounded place.

And when all else fails, I laugh. Yup...you heard me! I laugh! I mean...sometimes that is all you can do! The day that I stepped into a hallway full of water and couldn't take my students to their new classroom, I can't tell you how many times I laughed. The entire day was ridiculous! You couldn't make that story up!! All it took was a side glance from my friends and colleagues, and a giggle would erupt. But if I don't have someone to help me laugh, I find the laughs where I can by watching a funny show or even remembering something funny from the past. Laughing increases the brain's production of endorphins, which are feel-good chemicals that relieve pain and reduce stress. Laughter can lower our heart rate and blood pressure and can make us feel more relaxed. So yeah, when I feel like a Negative Nelly, sometimes getting myself to laugh is really the best medicine.

Practicing positivity is a conscious practice. It is habitual to be more positive and appreciative of all that is around me. This is hard stuff, which is why it takes purposeful and repeated practice over time. I'm not perfect at it, but I do like to say that I am a "work in progress." And I think with this, I really, truly mean it.

Being positive doesn't mean ignoring reality or making light of problems. It simply means that I approach the good and bad in life with the expectation that things will go well...or at least as best as I can make them.

I know, without a doubt in my mind, that **life is truly what we** *make of it.* Realizing this helps me choose to focus on and promote the positive in all aspects of my life.

Positive people live longer, suffer less medical illness, enjoy life more, have lower rates of depression and stress, feel well, and function better. Who wouldn't want that?? It sounds worth the practice to me, so I think I'll stick with it!

CHAPTER 52

to-do, to-don't, or to-be, that is the question

THIS MIGHT SOUND A LITTLE NUTTY TO SOME OF YOU, but I keep a daily list of tasks, commitments, and intentions—things I want to get done or accomplish. The list is usually fairly long, so I go a step further. I review my list and circle the most important things to do for the day. There is nothing I love more than crossing things off my list when I complete them. It gives me great satisfaction to not only see the circled items crossed off but to see my "bonus" things crossed off at the end of the day, as well! It is a GREAT day, and I feel very accomplished when that happens.

But sometimes, my to-do list dictates more about my day than I would like. At times, it can feel like it has its own voice, beckoning me to work harder, work faster, and **get things done**. Other times, it makes me feel defeated and unsatisfied because something got in the way of being able to cross a task off my list. The day can go from bad to worse when that happens.

That was me early last week. I sat down to begin my work day. I reviewed my list, adding things that I felt were important, circling my priority items, and getting ready to be the fantastic taskmaster that I am! But then I got interrupted. I honestly can't remember what got me this time, but I know that whatever it was, it kept me from digging into all that I planned to do that day.

One thing led to another, and my priority items went further and further down my to-do list. I kept coming back to my list, which is prominently tacked to a clipboard next to my computer, and I saw *nothing* that I had planned was getting done. I could feel my anxiety start to creep in. My heart raced, my breathing became shallow, and my eyeballs began to feel like they were bulging from my eye sockets (a true sign inside my body that I was feeling very overwhelmed).

At that point, I stopped. I turned my phone on silent. I turned the clipboard with my to-do list on it over so I couldn't see it. I closed my computer, and I went to lie down on my bed in silence for a few moments. And that is when it came to me....*I need to start writing a to-don't list.*

I don't know where this idea came from. I have never thought of or even heard of a "to-don't list." But I went back to my computer, opened Google, and searched how to write one. That's when I realized I'm not a genius. I didn't just discover a new "next best" thing! This has been done before. In fact, there are countless life hacks and articles written about the art of making a to-don't list. Even Oprah has tips on writing one! I felt like I hit the jackpot, and I couldn't wait to learn more!

First, I learned to think about time-wasters...things that easily distract me during valuable time blocks, especially those *mindless* activities. What takes away your productivity? For me, social media is definitely the problem! I have to promote my business on these platforms, so I can't just avoid them. However, I have to put some things on social media on hold until *after* my goals for the day have been completed. Another thing that stops my productivity is tidying. I work from home, and it is so easy for me to walk past the mess and have a compulsion to "just take a second" to pick it up. These tasks, like scrolling social media and cleaning, don't take a lot of brain power from me and often creep into my day because I'm not taking the real breaks that I actually need.

Second, I learned that my attachment to my "to-do" list isn't exactly healthy. One thing I need to add to this new list is "Don't spend too much time on your to-do list." Sounds crazy, right? But hear me out...sometimes, I spend too much time thinking about what I'm going to do and not actually doing it. It really shouldn't take me more than fifteen minutes a day to write, organize, and prioritize all that I have to do. If making a to-do list or revising my to-do list are items on my to-do list, I've just gone too far. It is time to spend less time thinking of getting things done and just get to it!

Next, upon deep examination of my habits, I realized that sometimes I put aside the needs of my loved ones for my to-do list. So, I learned that I need to add "don't ignore your loved ones, family, and friends, in spite of your busy day" to my to-don't list. Sometimes, I see a friend's number come up on my ringing phone, and I silence it because I just have too many things to do! Or, I'll cancel plans with a family member because my list is just too overwhelming. I'm embarrassed to admit that, and I'm not proud of it. I thrive on spending time with those that I love. They recharge me and give me the energy I need to keep going. If I put those that I love on hold or ignore them altogether because I'm *too busy*, I am going to start to resent my to-do list, and at that point, I may as well quit while I'm ahead!

Lastly, I realized through my research about to-don't lists that Elsa (from "Frozen") may have been on to something. Sometimes I just need to "Let it go!" My to-do list can make me feel like I need to be perfect and flawless. I need to let go of the perfectionism side of my brain. Yes...I want to strive to be my best. But being my best isn't always about crossing the items off my to-do list at the end of every day. I can prepare for a task, be ready for a challenge, do my research, and then be ready to move on.

Throughout my research about this new idea of a "to-don't list," I found a quote that really resonated with me...

> Remember the to-do lists,
> but don't forget the to-be list.
> —*Richard Branson*

And that's just it....it isn't about what I have to do or what I don't want to do. ***It is about what I want to be.*** What do I want people to say about me when I'm not in the room? How do I want to show up for my students, my friends, and my family? None of those answers are on my to-do or my to-don't list. That answer is within me, and it is clear as I go through my days creating, writing, teaching, and interacting with others.

I invite you to think not only about your to-do and your to-don't list...but your "to-be" list. When you're done reading this story, get out a piece of paper and write a list of adjectives you want people to use to describe you when you're not in the room. Write a list of things you can do to show up for everyone in your life, including yourself. And then go from there. At work, at home, with your loved ones, with your colleagues...how do you want to **BE**?

When you're done with that, get rid of your lists. Try a day without them. See where the day takes you. Spend time listening and looking around you to see what really **needs *your* attention.** I guarantee you'll be surprised at what will surface.

CHAPTER 53

the rollercoaster is real!

RECENTLY, I HAD THE HONOR OF PRESENTING MY "Emotions and Intentions" Wellness workshop to educators and staff at a local preschool. In my presentation, the hot topic of "burnout" came up. Burnout is a huge discussion piece not only in the education field but also in the rest of the world.

I think it is important to define what burnout really means. What is it, and how does it feel? According to the World Health Organization, burnout is defined as "chronic workplace stress that has not been successfully managed." Someone with burnout may feel:

Overwhelmed
Helpless
Overstimulated
Frustrated
Exhausted
Angry
Anxious
Numb

Hopeless
Depleted

These emotions are heavy and feel truly unpleasant when they all swirl together in our minds. But the reality is, many humans are walking the Earth feeling burnt out...feeling all the feels I've listed above and more. And many entities are quick to try to come up with solutions to the burnout. But I think we really need to talk about why the burnout is happening before we can try to solve it.

So, in my workshop this week with a local preschool, I gave a few reasons why many people, especially educators, are feeling all these feels:

Decision Fatigue
A constant state of fight or flight.
...and *emotional fatigue*.

Have you ever actually written down all the emotions you feel throughout the day? Maybe even just for an hour or two? Probably not....

That sounds a little crazy.
Who has time for that?

Whelp...I do, apparently. In all honesty, I took a class a few years ago where I was asked to list as many emotions as I could identify in a two-hour period throughout my day. This made me curious... do I really feel that much? I decided to write down all the emotions I could identify from the time I woke up in the morning to the time my students entered my classroom.

After going through the process, I surprised myself at how many emotions I felt in such a short amount of time. I was also shocked (but not really) about how my emotions were all over the place! I saw that one minute, I felt really pleasant. And then, in an instant, that feeling would morph into something very unpleasant. The energy level of my emotions bounced around from high to low throughout this time frame, as well.

It turns out that throughout this two-hour period, I could identify nine different emotions. That's roughly four emotions an hour or one emotion every fifteen minutes. To be honest, I *know* I felt more than that, but I wasn't really able to identify all the emotions at that time. When I look back, I can probably name about five to eight more feelings I experienced in addition to what I could identify.

With a variety of triggers in that two-hour period, I felt happy and determined. Then, I felt overwhelmed and disappointed, which quickly turned to relief and optimism...just to name a few.

I was sharing all of this with a group of teachers preparing to start the school year with their new students, and I could tell they could relate to the rollercoaster of emotions I was feeling a few years ago when I actually recorded them. Starting a new school year brings up more emotions than the average day for teachers and for everyone involved in the school and classroom:

Students
Parents
Principals
Custodians
Committee Chairs
School Secretaries

You name it, new school years bring up a lot of feelings for humans...and those emotions are all over the place.

This week, my daughter started seventh grade, and my son started his Sophomore year at a new high school. The levels of anxiety, worry, excitement, sadness, and more that they felt in the days leading up to and during the first week of school were *real*. And they were *valid*.

As a parent, I find myself strapped right next to my kids on their emotional rollercoasters. When they are worried, I worry for them. When they are sad, I'm sad for them. The hard part about this is that I am riding their rollercoaster and my rollercoaster *simultaneously*. This week, I was having big feelings about the school year starting, too:

I felt *nervous* about whether or not we made the right decision to send my son to a new school.

I felt *anxious* that my daughter's placement in her seventh-grade class might not have been the right fit.

I felt *apprehensive* and *stressed* about the changes in routine and schedules from summer to fall.

I felt *sad* that summer vacation was over.

I felt *proud* of my children.

I felt *hopeful* that everything would be OK.

I was feeling all of this on top of the big emotions I was having about work, my family, my home, and life in general! See what I mean? This week, my feelings were all over the place, and some of them even conflicted with each other! My own emotional rollercoaster is bumpy enough…to feel my kids' as well is downright exhausting.

Burnout-level exhausting.

But that is what we do as parents, right? It is part of the job. And I don't have a choice other than strapping on my seatbelt and holding on.

This, too, shall pass.

That's the thing about emotions…they come and go like waves on the ocean. They can arrive quickly and leave before you even have a chance to process what is happening. We can't avoid them, and they will hit us no matter what. But we do have a choice:

We can duck dive under them.
We can surf them.
We can brace ourselves.
We can let them knock us down.

I'm not saying that burnout is a choice. But I will say that we have many options for how we want to manage all the emotions on the burnout rollercoaster. After all, according to the World Health Organization, burnout occurs when "stress" (aka emotions) isn't properly managed.

That was the message that I was trying to convey in my workshop at the preschool this week. I wanted my fellow educators to know all the feelings that go into being an educator (AND a human):

Are *real,* and they are *valid.*
And we can learn and use more tools to help move us through them.

This goes for those of us working outside the field of education as well. We aren't born learning how to manage our emotions. As humans, we need to feel them, name them, express them, and manage them. This is a learned process that takes time, practice, and lots of mistake-making. It is a life-long school of learning.

Putting feelings into words can actually reduce the force of unpleasant emotions. As I've heard many professionals in the field of psychology say,

> "You have to name it, to tame it."

Feel it, to heal it.
Recognize it, to humanize it.

The one thing that educators, parents, and human beings in general have in common is that along with having jobs to do, we also have lives that include families, relationships, work, trauma, and more! We ALL need tools and strategies for managing all that life brings us. Or we will, for sure, suffer from burnout.

Somedays, we have nice, calm, lapping waves of emotions. In others, the waves hit us like the sea in a hurricane. Understanding that *the rollercoaster is* **REAL** and extending grace, patience, and understanding to ourselves and others will help us navigate life's challenges more smoothly.

CHAPTER 54

mental health days

I FEEL ENTIRELY OVERWHELMED.

Between my family schedule and all I have to do for work, I just can't keep up. I just have too many things on my shoulders.

I have been walking around with a chronic headache for a week. Stress eating doesn't even begin to describe the binges I've gone on lately. I cry at the drop of a hat, and I'm just plain exhausted.

Yet every day, I wake up early so I can do a workout and get myself ready for the day before I need to get my kids up and running. I do my work in between school drop-offs and pickups. Then, I spend my afternoons running in different directions while squeezing as much of my work as possible. I plan and cook dinners. I pack lunches. I keep up with my inbox, which is full of school news and upcoming events. My calendar is so packed that I have to scroll down on my phone to see it all. I don't think I've stopped in months.

This pace is making me sick. I wish I had a day where I could just be alone with my thoughts. I wish I could take an hour or two to just be lazy, read a book, or watch TV. I wish I could do my workouts well after the sun was up, at a more human-like hour. I wish I had a day where I didn't have a list of things to do or a schedule to keep.

Wait...why couldn't I?

When I taught in a public school classroom, I was too afraid to take a mental health day from school. There was always too much to do. Sometimes, I felt that if I took a day off, it would put me back a week and end up giving me more work. Even writing sub plans for the teacher who would take my classroom for the day made it feel like a day off wasn't worth it.

Sometimes, we think that working hard to the point of exhaustion makes us better and stronger. Go ahead and reread that paragraph where I described the sensations I felt at being overwhelmed. Nothing in that description makes it sound like I was showing up as my best self for anyone.

There is no shame in taking a mental health day.
Let me repeat that in a different way.
There is no reason why taking a mental health day is the wrong thing to do.

I work hard both at home and at my job. My family and my students know that. If I take a short break to work on my own well-being once in a while, I will gain the strength to continue to help everyone thrive.

The other day, with these thoughts in mind, I rearranged some clients, rewrote my to-do list to push some tasks for later in the week, and enlisted other adults in my life to help take care of my kids.

And I took care of myself.

I woke up at the same time as my kids; I gave them breakfast, helped them pack their bags, and drove them where they needed to be.

And then the day was mine! I drove to the beach and took a walk...my exercise for the day. I sat for a bit and read my book. I stopped at a farm stand for a fresh and healthy lunch. I didn't need to rush home because I knew my husband was going to take care of picking the kids up in the afternoon.

Did I still have responsibilities? Yes! I picked up some dinner rations at the farm stand while I was there. But here's the difference...I was so relaxed at the end of the day that I actually enjoyed cooking it. I packed lunches for the next day. And I helped my kids with their homework.

And the whole entire time, I felt present and content.

My headache was gone. I didn't stress eat even once! And I slept like a champ.

When I woke up the next morning, I felt ready for whatever the day had in store for me.

There's value in the time I gave myself. How can I show up for others when I'm not showing up for myself?

In a job where I take care of everyone else, I now see how important it is to remember to take care of myself, too.

My overwhelming feelings were making me sick...just like any cold or virus would do. We stay home when we have a fever. Why can't we do the same when we feel mentally drained?

I just realized that I can.

And trust me, it was worth every effort.

postscript

I KNOW I AM A FORTUNATE HUMAN BEING! I HAVE AN amazing family and a great group of friends. I have an extraordinary village of people around me who pick me up when I'm down, inspire me, and show me more love and care than I sometimes deserve. I am realizing as I get older that *everyone is dealing with something*. Some things are really big, and others are small and trivial. And these things ebb and flow as life continues to go on around us. If we didn't have each other to bounce ideas off of, laugh with, and vent to, I am not sure any of us would make it through this conflicted world. We need other humans in our lives.

The problem is that many of us don't *really* like to talk about how we *truly* feel. And sometimes it feels uncomfortable when someone shares their big feelings. Writing these stories of small moments in my life and expressing my feelings and emotions about it all is not easy. At times, it can feel embarrassing, shameful, and sometimes downright raw to put it all on paper. However, I chose to write all these stories with educators, parents, and caregivers in mind to get the narrative started among all of us. No matter what we look like, who we vote for, what we do for a living, or where we reside, we have something in common. And that is that we are all trying to navigate through our days with ourselves, our families, and our loved ones by our sides.

> We all want to feel cared for and accepted.
> We all want to be successful.
> We all want what is best for those we love.
> And none of us are perfect at any of it!

We are human.

We are learning as we go, with every new experience, at all ages. None of us were born with a manual telling us what to do and how to act in every situation that life throws at us. We want our children to have long, healthy, and successful lives. And since they aren't born with manuals either, we need to teach them what we know. This is why I shared a few of my stories from the course of about a year here in this book.

Our world needs more reminders of how we can all *be unequivocally human*. My hope is that through my stories, my readers can see that there is a lesson in everything that nature throws at us. The world can use a little more time to reflect on how to better manage emotions and live together in a community. We can all take a little more time to nurture ourselves so that we can better take care of the members of our own villages.

Social-emotional learning is life-long learning. It never ends. With every experience and every mistake, it is important to reflect and reevaluate how we want to show up for ourselves and others as we continue to move forward. How we relate to others, how we make decisions, having social and self-awareness, having emotional intelligence, and being able to manage it are all the skills that makeup SEL. I truly believe that these skills are something ALL humans need to learn at any age and stage. And if we explicitly teach humans at a young age, we can help them grow even more resilient and strong than we are as adults. Working on these skills for ourselves and everyone we care for is the way we can build a better world for all!

With the heart of an educator, I can't help but leave all of you with this thought by Italian writer Cesare Pavese:

"Lessons are not given, they are taken."

My biggest hope and dream is that in this life, we all do everything we can to understand the lessons that life offers us so that together, we can *be well, my friends.*

acknowledgments

WHEN I WAS WORKING AS A PUBLIC SCHOOL TEACHER, a colleague of mine, who worked heavily in the SEL realm with us, wrote an email to our staff every week that she titled "TGIF." The email usually had some sort of story, quote, or anecdote to wrap up the week and inspire us before heading into the weekend. When she left that position, I loved it so much that I decided to continue the tradition. I had no idea who read it and if my colleagues had enjoyed it (or felt annoyed by it!). But I loved writing it so much, I didn't want to stop! I started to realize that writing these things felt healing to me.

That is when my "Calm Blog" was born! When I left the public school classroom and started my business, I began to write a blog post every Friday on my website. In keeping with tradition, I always write "TGIF" at the start of every social media post containing my blog. And I always sign it, "Be well, my friends."

For an entire year, I wrote a blog post a week expressing lessons I learned from real-life events. I recently decided to take all these blog posts (and more!) and turn them into a book to share with as many people as possible. I always dreamed of being an author, and now here I am...but I didn't do it without the help of a whole bunch of special people in my life. In the spirit of writer and philosopher Voltaire, who said,

> "Appreciation is a wonderful thing. It makes what is excellent in others belong to us as well."

...I'd like to take a moment to thank those who have gotten me to this point in my life.

A huge hug and thank you to my husband, Andrew. When I left teaching, you encouraged me to take a HUGE leap with an even bigger pay cut! I can't thank you enough for entertaining my crazy idea to tweak my career and motivating me to keep going. I love you more than you know!

Thank you to my kids, Jack and Ella. You two are the most inspiring people that I have in my life. I love watching you grow, change, and learn. I am so grateful to be your mom, and I'm immensely proud of everything you do every day. I love you!

I don't even want to know what my parents and sister were thinking and feeling when I called them and told them I was leaving my teaching position of over twenty years to start this crazy journey as an SEL coach and now an author. As a parent myself, I can imagine it wasn't easy to be supportive of such a big change! A giant thank you to my parents and my sister, Kim, for *always* supporting me and cheering me on. I love you guys!

A special thanks to my friend, Jen Daniels. You were the one who listened to me when I cried about my stress and worry in my public school teaching career and reminded me that I could do hard things. If it wasn't for your talk with me that day over brunch, I wouldn't have had the courage to be where I am today. I love you, my friend!

To my friend, Cara Sanchez, who left this world too soon. Thank you for joining me at the start of my SEL journey. I will be forever grateful for every moment that we practiced yoga, meditated, breathed, and worked through the hard emotions together. I am where I am today because of our work together. I miss you, my friend.

To another friend gone too soon, Katie Carey. Thank you for being a great colleague and, more importantly, my confidant. I would never have gotten through the hard days in the classroom if it wasn't for you. You made me a better teacher, and I am so honored I got to teach with you for more than half my career in a public school classroom. I miss you.

I don't know where I would be without any of my friends! To all of you out there who have encouraged me along the way, listened to and supported all of my ideas about teaching, parenting, and life in general. I am forever grateful for each and every one of you. It makes me happy when you ask me questions about what I'm doing and when you share what I do with others. You talk me through the ups and downs of life and give me so much inspiration. I hope I am as good of a friend to you as you are to me! I can't thank you enough!

To my colleagues in education, especially those who work in the Barrington Public Schools, where I worked for most of my career... You are all amazing teachers with so much to offer our younger generations. Keep doing what you are doing because the world needs more of you in it! Thank you for your continued support and for cheering me on with every new development in my career change.

To all of my childhood teachers—thank you! Each of you has given me a little bit to get me to where I am today. I love to write because of my English teachers. I love to teach because you were such amazing models. I am one of the many products of your labor, and I am so grateful to all of you!

And finally, to my readers. Thank you for riding on this journey along with me in this book. I hope you were able to find meaning, insight, and growth between the pages to take into your own lives.

ABOUT THE AUTHOR
Jenny Gaynor, MEd, RYT

Photo by Casey Henchman

JENNY GAYNOR, AUTHOR AND FOUNDER of Calm Education, works with children, families, and teachers to teach SEL (Social Emotional Learning) skills. The mission of her business, Calm Education, is to bring SEL techniques and strategies to children, their families, and their teachers for the promotion of self-confidence, healthy connections to others, and resiliency so everyone can contribute to a more emotionally intelligent world!

Jenny is a former educator. She worked as an elementary classroom teacher for over 20 years in Rhode Island, Massachusetts, and California. She currently holds both elementary educator (grades 1-6) and special educator (grades K-12) certifications. She earned an Undergraduate Degree in English and Elementary Education from the University of Rhode Island and a Master's Degree in Special Education from Rhode Island College. Jenny has an extensive background in a variety of SEL techniques and programs, such as Responsive Classroom and RULER. She also holds a 200-hour yoga teacher certificate and SEL Facilitator certificate from "Breathe for Change," and she has training in meditation and breathwork.

Jenny lives in Barrington, RI, with her husband, Andrew, her two children, Jack and Ella, and her unofficial therapy cat, Tiller.

www.ingramcontent.com/pod-product-compliance
Lightning Source LLC
Chambersburg PA
CBHW071110160426
43196CB00013B/2525